Nightingales, Bluebirds & Angels of Mercy

True Stories of the Courage and Heroism of Nurses on the Front Line in WWII

Elise Baker

Table of Contents

Introduction

I attribute my success to this: I never gave nor took any excuse.
—Florence Nightingale

Before the World Wars, nursing was seen as a lowly job. It was a selfless and difficult career to pursue, and nurses often sacrificed "the good life" to help others. Much like a nun, they were perceived as sacrosanct in their duty, a figure of piety and hardship. Nursing certainly was not a role that many families approved of as a "first choice" for their daughters.

In general, nurses put their desire for marriage, children, and comfort below their duty to serve. This did not mean that the typical nurse rejected those normal aspects of womanhood, it solely meant that she decided to set them aside, at least for a time. Nurses became the small percentage of women who chose to deviate from traditional expectations to more decisive and empowered actions. The Great War (WWI) started to change perceptions of nurses slowly. Because nurses were suddenly desperately needed and in short supply, they started to become a bit more recognized and appreciated during that time.

The famous British nurse, Florence Nightingale, took 19th-century ideas of nursing and healthcare and made the profession cleaner, safer, and more pragmatic for patients and staff alike. In World War II (WWII), frontline nurses continued the legacy of Florence Nightingale, known as "the Lady with the Lamp."

Female nurses in history have always been presented in a supportive and nurturing role, assisting male doctors and surgeons, subserviently following behind the troops. And while that's true, they also contributed a great deal in shaping modern medicine and patient care. And some were quite bold.

Florence Nightingale broke the mold—her voice and actions her greatest tools. A woman speaking up was looked down upon in the realms of men, especially in the field of medicine. Florence Nightingale stood above the rest in her pursuit to change minds and build stronger ideals around the profession of nursing and female intelligence in general. The goal was for nursing to become a profession in which women were respected and cherished for their intelligence and their work, not solely because they were "natural caretakers."

But as the World Wars raged and nurses continued to focus on proper training, hygiene, and professionalism, the value of their positions increased. Nurses were saving lives and it was slowly becoming an honor to be one. No longer a symbol of pity, a nurse became a symbol of dedication and upstanding citizenry. Consequently, more women decided to don their nurse caps and capes. And this sentiment did not just pervade the field of nursing, but far more male-dominated fields as well.

Those tumultuous six years of WWII gave women a break from tradition and elevated their capability in the eyes of men, and most importantly, in their own eyes. While this nascent movement started in WWI on a very small scale in different pockets of the world, as WWII loomed and got bigger, so did the need to fill gaps in the workforce as more and more men enlisted in war efforts.

Women famously assumed the mantle of factory worker, driver, pilot, mechanic, mapper, and builder while retaining their traditional roles as mother, sister, daughter, and wife at home. Women volunteered in every niche and gap that could be found. They even infiltrated the secretive world of cryptology in the war, assisted in spy operations, and helped engineer various projects in computers and warfare mechanics.

However, the majority of women, working or not, remained close to home, still relatively far away from enemy lines. On the home front, they heard of the war through their relatives and via daily radio transmissions and news. Although they heard all about men dying on the battlefields and the ever-changing politics of war, the average woman stayed safe at home.

In stark contrast to women at home were military nurses within the Army, Navy, or Air Force—the closest a woman could get to the front lines. Combat nurses stood apart from the General Hospital (GH) nurses in safer Allied cities that received patients both from the field and within their civilian walls. Many military nurses, called combat nurses or field nurses, were already qualified before the war arrived, and many took up nursing solely because the war was upon them.

In 1939 within many of the Allied nations, there arose a sudden need to recruit nurses. A huge portion of funding was directed to training efforts because nations were in absolute dire need to expand healthcare. By

1941, their staffing count had fallen dangerously short of the projected numbers of injured soldiers.

If you had the guts, the stamina, and the sheer nerve to do a job despite enemy planes flying overhead, or enemy troops shooting a mile away, or the possibility of being captured and taken prisoner, then you could well be drafted straight into the action! In fact, field nurses saw the war far sooner than other women, as they were on the battlefield before females were technically allowed in the military.

Trained by the experienced women and men who served in WWI, this next generation of military nurses—the first to be ranked—would operate in all branches of the military. In Army, Navy, and Air Force units stationed all around the globe, they followed their Allied troops and faced the remnants of battle with a decisive plan. Their quiet strength and bravery were not truly validated in comparison to the glory and fanfare received by homecoming troops after the war ended.

WWII brought nurses into the trenches, into the mud and cold of the European theater, into the harsh and unforgiving climate of North Africa, and the wet jungles of Southeast Asia. Nurses would train like the men, eat like the men, and live like the men until the job was done.

They were away for years on end, with little time to write home to their mothers or their serving sweethearts. Those at sea had their precious mail delayed for months. Those in prison camps were cut off completely. Yet nurses rushed to enlist for military service in their thousands, spurred by the same impulses as their male compatriots—a sense of duty and a desire for adventure. They faced long hauls over open waters and confronted enemy forces head-on; some faced the unendurable and lived to tell their tale.

The nurse subsequently became the greatest symbol of hope for all during the trauma of two world wars.

And that is where this book, part of the *Brave Women Who Changed the Course of WWII* series, addresses the remarkable lack of attribution to female characters who entered the World Wars due to the conflict of men, but who left it changed, sometimes for the better, for the struggle they endured, and sometimes for the worse because they were soon to be forgotten as their achievements were acknowledged far too late, if ever.

Redressing the balance of historical data to reflect a more accurate view of the achievements of the women heroes of WWII is essential, both in understanding the past and looking to the future.

This book illuminates the nurse on the front line as a hero in her own right as she treated the wounded whilst under fire, put her own life at risk, and made life-and-death decisions on the spot. She was maimed, imprisoned, and killed. She suffered from fatigue, sickness, and tropical disease alongside her male counterparts.

Not only did the combat nurse deal with the horrific battlefield wounds of frontline warfare, but they also had to do battle with the entrenched male chauvinism of the military, fighting for recognition of their rank, their career progression, and their remuneration. Poor and sporadic pay also meant that they often couldn't afford to buy even basic necessities, while the orderlies ranking below them were paid their full military salary each month. A sure sign of the value of their sex.

Who can say what the world might have looked like at the end of WWII had women not stood up to be counted? Who can measure the ways countless lives, saved by the efforts of the combat nurse, went on to contribute to society?

This is not a patriotic account of nurses who served a single country or army but a celebration of the nurses who represented the Allied forces, regardless of borders or nationality.

The book's title refers to terms such as "Angels of Mercy" and "Nightingales," which have been ascribed, in a variety of combinations, to nurses throughout modern history. Air ambulance nursing crews, for example, became known as "The Flying Angels," whereas the "Bluebirds" are uniquely Canadian.

These untold stories of female heroes of WWII illustrate the true meaning of sacrifice, from the gender that was barred from taking a fellow human's life on the front lines of war but was allowed to instead give it back graciously, one tender touch at a time, wielding the instruments of healing rather than those of destruction.

Peppered throughout the facts are pieces of their stories that were influenced by films, books, interviews, and even imagination. We can't know everything these brave women did and thought, so occasional liberties are taken to fill out their stories, all in keeping with what is known of their lives and personalities.

Recognition of the WWII military nurse is long overdue. This book shines a spotlight on the true stories of Allied combat nurses, their courage, and their compassion. It is high time their names were brought out of the shadows and into the light of public awareness. Some have well-documented early years, while others have obscure pasts, but their collective message reads clearly: Bravery together!

Let's meet our heroes from the United States, the United Kingdom, Australia, and Canada.

The Americans: Army Nursing Corps (ANC)

1. Katherine Nolan
2. Marcella LeBeau

The British and Australians: Queen Alexandra's Royal Imperial Nurse Corps (QAs) and the Australian Army Nurse Corps (AANC)

3. Margot Turner
4. Vivian Bullwinkel

The Canadians: Royal Canadian Army Medical Corps (RCAMC)

5. Jessie Middleton & Elizabeth Lowe

Welcome to the story of female nurses in World War II. While many people seem to know they existed, very few observed their sacrifice and courage in such perilous times of war. Before we delve into the lives of our two Americans, we will explore the body under which they served—The American Army Nurse Corps.

Acronyms & Definitions

Hospital Designations

- **FH**—Field Hospital: Mobile hospital
- **EH**—Evacuation Hospital
- **SH**—Station Hospital
- **GH**—General Hospital

Field Hospitals (FH) and *Evacuation Hospitals (EH)* had to be mobile in order to follow advancing troops. FHs were located closest to the front lines so soldiers could be brought over as quickly as possible. EHs were typically set up further away from the action for safety, but close enough for reasonable transport. Their typical construction was canvas tents, but whenever possible, staff would also try to secure schools, barracks, hospital buildings, hotels, large homes, or any physical structure that was both suitable and available. Before a unit was set to move, the hospital stopped admitting new patients and relocated their existing patients to nearby hospitals. Crews would load equipment and personnel into trucks, move to the next designated location, and set up shop. They were ready to accept patients within hours. When EHs had to be broken down and moved, patients were sent by whatever means possible (ambulance, plane, train, or ship) to more permanent locations within the theater of war, such as the *Station Hospitals (SH)* or *General Hospitals (GH)* in main cities nearby. There they would get surgery and convalesce. Because brick and mortar hospital buildings weren't always an option, especially in tropical locations, some SHs were a collection of temporary buildings.

POW—Prisoner of War

A *Prisoner of War (POW)* is considered to be any person captured or interned by a hostile power during war. International conferences at the Hague in 1899 and again in 1907 established rules of conduct that became somewhat recognized in international law. Because there were millions of POWS in WWI that were not well-treated, the issue was revisited in 1929 at the Geneva Convention. The convention established that prisoners of war were to be removed from the battle and treated humanely; it was ratified by many nations (US, UK, France, etc.), but not by Japan or the Soviet Union.

Millions of people were taken prisoner in WWII; some experienced very good treatment while others experienced quite the opposite (Britannica, 2021):

> The United States and Great Britain generally maintained the standards set by the Hague and Geneva conventions in their treatment of Axis POWs. Germany treated its British, French, and American prisoners comparatively well but treated Soviet, Polish, and other Slavic POWs with genocidal severity. ... The Japanese treated their British, American, and Australian POWs

harshly, and only about 60 percent of these POWs survived the war. After the war, international war crimes trials were held in Germany and Japan, based on the concept that acts committed in violation of the fundamental principles of the laws of war were punishable as war crimes. (para. 7)

RN —Registered Nurse

A *Registered Nurse (RN)* is a nurse who has graduated from an accredited institution in a given state, province, or country and has met the requirements by that licensing body to be granted a nursing license.

World War II Nursing Units

- **ANC**—Army Nursing Corps (United States)

- **AANC**—Australian Army Nurse Corps

- **QAs**—Queen Alexandra's Royal Imperial Nurse Corps (Britain)

- **RCAMC**—Royal Canadian Army Medical Corps

The American Army
Nurse Corps

Creation of the ANC

After the infamous bombing of Pearl Harbor by the Japanese at the end of 1941, the world changed dramatically. The American government immediately stood up the Army Nurse Corps (ANC) to post nurses in the Hawaiian region. Six months later, the government department had grown from 1,000 enrollments to 12,000.

To enroll in the ANC, a woman had to meet certain basic requirements:

- be 21-45 years of age (increased from 40 years after 1941),

- be single (unmarried),

- have no children younger than 14,

- have graduated from high school and nursing school (licensed),

- be certified as physically healthy,

- be a US citizen,

- be of sound mind with moral and ethical traits backed up by relative testimonial, and

- maintain a professional demeanor.

Other Allied nations would soon adopt similar requirements for their own units.

Nursing Propaganda

How do you recruit 11,000 nurses in six months? Create a lot of fanfare and propaganda and advertise like crazy. In the US, that's exactly what the government did.

"Make Nursing Your War Job" and "Save his life… and find your own" were two of the many slogans printed on posters, newspapers, and magazines aimed at young women in 1940.

The nicknames "Angels of Mercy" or "Nightingales" used in WWII allude to the original angel of mercy, Florence Nightingale. You will notice in the following chapters that the cherished nicknames of these nurse units from various Allied countries always referenced the humility and grace of the 19th-century nurse and the magnanimous contribution she made to the profession across the world.

The propaganda of the time often portrayed the delightful aspects of joining the war, shining a softer light on the many scary and unforgiving aspects of military nursing. This subtle false advertisement would be the great call to action that young, ambitious women followed. The messages glamorized travel, personal growth, camaraderie, and career.

- Travel the world seeing, tasting, and learning new things.

- Work with the best staff and equipment money can buy.

- Grow in spirit and maturity along with thousands of other nurses.

- Create camaraderie with nursing sisters you could never experience at home.

Military Training

Many of the women applying to the ANC had no military training and did not understand army lingo or procedures. They were primarily recruited through the American Red Cross and were drafted into General Hospitals (GH), Station Hospitals (SH), Evacuation Hospitals (EH), or Field Hospitals (FH).

By 1943, the nursing shortage would call for women to become not only a nurse on the ground, but also in the sky and on the water, through Flight Hospitals (nurses working on planes) and Hospital Ships (nurses working on cruisers).

These WWII Nursing Sisters, named for nuns around the world who had traditionally practiced hospital care centuries earlier, were now more involved than their predecessors ever were. They were expected to go above and beyond bedside care, taking on Officer status, but still preferring to be called Sister.

"Prior to 1943, nurses were not required to have any special military training, but this changed in July of that year" (*Nursing and medicine*, 2014). The commissioning of army nurses required them to complete extra training in field medical service setup and sanitation, which heavily depended on the area in which they were being sent, for example, the jungles of Malaya were quite different from the arid deserts in North Africa. They were required to build physical strength and endurance, while still focusing on the administration of anesthetics and some psychiatry for patients and fellow nurses.

Keeping up the morale of the unit and the patients in the ward was exceptionally important. These new skills were eagerly taught and surely something an average nurse would have never been able to learn within the confines of her hospital at home.

Upon induction into the ANS, the women held their right hands over their hearts and pledged together (*Pledge of the U.S. Army Nurse, World War II*, 2007):

> As an Army nurse, I accept the responsibilities of an officer in the Army Nurse Corps.
>
> I shall give faithful care to the men who fight for the freedom of this Country and to the women who stand behind them.
>
> I shall bring to the American soldier, wherever he may be, the best of my knowledge and professional skill.
>
> I shall approach him cheerfully at all times, under any conditions I may find.
>
> I shall endeavor to maintain the highest nursing standards possible in the performance of my duties.

I shall appear fearless in the presence of danger and quiet the fears of others to the best of my ability.

My only criticism shall be constructive. The reputation and good name of the Army Nurse Corps and of the nursing profession shall be uppermost in my thoughts, second only to the care of my patients.

I shall endeavor to be a credit to my country and to the uniform I wear.

Nurses of Color

While the army was desperately in need of more nurses, racism was still a major factor for young African American nurses, and as we will see in Chapter 2, Native Americans too.

During the 1940s, people in power still assigned value to the color of your skin. Only in 1944 did the US government open military service to African American women via the ANC. It was initially limited to 500 African American nurses in the army, which paled in comparison to the thousands who were willing and able to serve. Disgracefully, only four African American women were ever posted in the navy.

Nurses of color were mainly restricted to working in their segregated hospitals and looking after their African American compatriots, but they were also considered *appropriate* to treat German POWs. The army was also worried about the possibility of nurses and German POWs getting too friendly with each other. The belief at the time, incredible as it now seems, was that there would be less risk of romantic and sexual liaisons between German POWs and Black nurses. "It felt like a betrayal to be assigned to care for enemy soldiers instead of wounded American soldiers" (*African American nurses*, 2019).

Those first few nurses of color who were sent overseas, specifically to England, were welcomed by Brigadier General Benjamin O'Davis, who happened to be the first African American general in the US Army, with this statement (*The Second World War*, 2015):

> I am told that you are the first colored nurses to come to this area. I know that you are going to live up to all of the traditions of your noble profession, and the American people expect great things of you.

It seems that the government knew how to enlist their service but cared little for the potential they truly had. American nurses before 1942 held what was called "relative rank." "They held the title, wore the insignia, were admitted to officers' clubs, and had the privilege of the salute, but they had limited authority in the line of duty and initially received less pay than men of similar rank" (Sundin, 2018a). Only in 1944 were American nurses fully recognized and subsequently authorized to receive full pay and military privileges.

The Issue of Sex

Sex was a highly charged issue in all the theater of war. Whether nurses fell in love (or lust) with patients, fellow doctors, assisting soldiers, or locals in the country where they worked, intercourse occurred, despite being considered improper. But the constant proximity to death, danger, and destruction lent wartime romances and sexual encounters a particular urgency.

In an NPR radio interview for her 2013 book, *What Soldiers Do: Sex and the American GI in World War II France*, historian Mary Louise Roberts says:

> It was a particularly eroticized war. Anybody who remembers the pinups on airplanes, Rita Hayworth, the amount to which pinups became a part of the culture of the GIs, will recognize to what extent sex became important to the war experience. I went and looked at Stars and Stripes, which is the trench journal, and what I saw there was an extension of the pinup culture. Photojournalism in particular was used to portray the French woman as ready to be rescued, ready to greet the American soldier and ready to congratulate and thank him through a kiss or even more.

Most Allied governments considered getting pregnant an infraction, with immediate removal from the corps. Getting married also meant a woman had to relinquish her duties. Removed from the danger zone, she was expected to take on the traditional role of wife with her new husband, even if he was off fighting the war.

Many rules around female modesty governed nursing schools and military training. A nurse's rank in hospitals was purportedly given to dissuade lower-ranking male officers from even speaking to the army nurse, much less flirting with them. Again, this was considered to be a "protection" for nurses in order to reduce unwanted advances by lowly enlisted men.

"However, the sense of prudishness perpetuated by long skirts and separate spheres was made irrelevant when it came to saving soldiers. A woman must soar beyond the conventional modesty considered correct under different circumstances" (Jensen, 2017).

By the end of the war in 1945, around 59,000 women had joined the ANC. This was a collaboration of people from all over the country, all with one purpose and agenda.

In the next two chapters, we will meet two young American women who more than found their footing in the nursing profession—Kate Nolan and Marcella LeBeau.

Chapter 1:

Katherine Nolan

Her room is small but cozy, a place she has called her own all these years. She busies herself while listening to her favorite jazz pieces on vinyl—the likes of Tony Scott, Stan Levy, and Charlie Parker. While she listens to the soft music, she packs her most important belongings. She is excited but mostly anxious about what's to come.

Never before has she traveled and never before has she heard of so much widespread destruction and human need. Yet she still smiles to herself, happy to start her adventure, not so sure when and how she will return. She supposes that this is the bittersweet part of being a combat nurse as a young adult.

Saying goodbye to her mother, promising her that she will be home soon, kissing her on her cheek, and wiping away her tears is the hardest thing she has ever had to do. Saying goodbye to her soft bed, her favorite food, her habitual and effortless ease... but she has bigger things to do now.

She knows the trip is long, dangerous, and oftentimes unpredictable. She also knows she will see things she has never before imagined, but that she *will have* to be ready. Whether she likes it or not, this is what she signed up for. And who is she to be afraid when thousands more are dying and in desperate need of her help?

The Venture

Figure 1: First Lieutenant Katherine (Flynn) Nolan, US Army Nurse Corps, WWII

Credit to Women in Military Service for America Memorial Foundation, Inc.

Katherine Flynn Nolan was born in America, in the large city of Worcester in the state of Massachusetts, a few years after the Great War (WWI) in 1920. Not too much is known about her parents, but we can gather that she spent her happy childhood within an average middle-class family, in an average middle-class suburb on the East Coast.

WWI certainly had an impact on young Kate's life. Some of her family members, like her uncle, served and came home as veterans, while others never returned. Therefore, like many of the nurses before and after her, the stories of despair from WWI were a great catalyst for her to qualify and practice nursing later on.

Nolan attended Hahnemann Hospital in Worcester for her training as a nurse, receiving her registered nurse license (RN) in April of 1943 at the age of 23. A few months after that, she enlisted in the Army Nurse Corps (ANC).

That very year, a bill was established allowing a special government program to assist and accelerate nurse training—the Nurse Training Act. The faster nurses were able to get their licenses, the faster they were able to help in the field, and thus President Roosevelt signed off on the act in July 1943. The act incentivized nursing schools all across the country to take part by providing funding for accredited nursing schools to ensure that all applicants took part in the Cadet Nurse Corps. This federal training program assisted the US government in relieving the Nursing Schools of much-needed staff and training separately to speed up qualification and posting.

"Applicants would be granted subsidization of nursing school tuition, associated expenses, and a shorter training period. In exchange, applicants pledged to actively serve in essential civilian or other federal government services for the duration of the war"

(Hitchcock, 2018). By the time the war ended, 1,125 of the 1,300 nursing schools in the US had affiliated themselves with the program.

Capable Kate

As Nolan had attended her nursing school before this act was established, her acceptance into the ANC was as swift as breath; the wartime vacuum sucked her in.

While she was a little late to the party, as the war had been raging for some time already, nevertheless, she would be front and center for the last push. Her accounts in journals and interviews give us straightforward facts about her career and progress throughout the war.

Nolan was immediately stationed at MacDill Army Air Field in Tampa, Florida for her four-week formal military orientation and training. The base was a major air defense for the Gulf of Mexico against the unyielding German U-boat (submarine) attacks on the Atlantic. What she couldn't know was that a year from this very training, she would be standing in the fields of war, soaked and tired. Instead, she remained exuberant in her new position and in the *not knowing*.

Nolan received her basic military behavior training, mapping, camouflage, radio communication, and field equipment training at MacDill Army Air Field Base (AFB), Interestingly enough, in 1943, two films were shot on the AFB. The young women who were training there would often sneak away to see if they could catch a glimpse of any famous actors.

Apart from trying to suss out who was starring in which movie, Nolan (then Flynn) would soon catch the eye of an officer, a certain James Nolan, who also resided and worked at the airbase. They became fast friends, despite it being a strange time when no real commitments could be made due to their assigned postings and the uncertainty about whether they'd return home. Nevertheless, they maintained correspondence over the years, building a budding romance through letters.

When the month-long training at MacDill AFB was complete, Nolan was assigned to the 53rd Field Hospital (FH) unit and sent south to Fort Bragg, North Carolina to join them. Now a combat nurse and a Second Lieutenant, she knew her individual duties, but she still needed to learn how to work as a team with the rest of the doctors, nurses, and orderlies in her unit.

At Fort Bragg, she continued to learn army lingo, train in harder routes, and hike farther distances with packs and pretend cargo, adjusting herself to the overall army routine. All new recruits needed these skills to be drilled over and over until they dreamed about them at night. This was especially the case with those enlisted in field sanitation, ward management, and tent setup and breakdown.

"Every day in this new world brought a dizzying array of new experiences. Her uniform was stiff, scratchy, and smelled like mothballs. The Army boots were new and too tight" (Eder, 2021). Her days were full of tasks and stress as she conformed to the duties of Lieutenant. She needed to pick up the pace, and fast!

"Lieutenant Flynn!" screams a commanding officer at the training base just as she stepped out of her quarters for the morning drill.

"Sir yes Sir," she quickly replies, stiffening her back, keeping her knees and ankles firmly together, and placing her right hand above her brow in a typical salute while staring straight ahead.

"Something is missing from your uniform this morning, Lieutenant. Can you tell me what that is?" the male officer says, staring at her in obvious irritation and expecting a quick reply.

Nolan thinks hard for a second or two, noticing his eyes roaming the top of her head. *Oh, shoot! My silly hat!* she suddenly remembers, blushing. "Sir, I believe I have forgotten to place a hat on my head," she replies rather sheepishly.

"Well spotted, Lieutenant," he retorts sarcastically. "Now, scoot! Morning drill is in five and do not let me catch you without your cap again."

Apart from understanding uniform etiquette, Nolan also had to learn how to identify friendly from enemy aircraft by carefully listening to the engine of the plane passing overhead. She knew the Allied planes used a Rolls Royce engine, which sounded a lot smoother than those of German or Japanese aircraft.

Before she left for duty later that year, she was given a poem titled "A Goodbye Poem" by Morris Kleinman, who joyfully wrote (Stamberg, 2004):

This is about a girl I've seen,

She works all night in Ward fifteen.

She's small, she's cute, she's pretty thin,

With the Irish name of Katherine Flynn.

Her army rank makes her a Louey,

When asked about it, she answers phooey.

She likes her job and will not quit,

Until the enemy ranks are split.

This freckle-face doll is a lady of class,

Another good Irishman from Worcester, Mass.

While Kleinman turned out to be an unsavory character, his adorable poem sheds a little more light on Nolan's character and perseverance.

In her 1996 book, *No Time for Fear: Voices of American Nurses in World War II*, Diane Fessler creates a comprehensive picture of what happened behind the curtain of war. The American HQ made extensive plans and facilitated complex logistics in order to manage people and equipment. For example, they needed to post nurses, replace them when necessary, track their ever-changing locations, log their hours on duty, and ensure they had food, personal gear, hospital equipment, and medical supplies to do their jobs. Fessler writes:

> When the invasion of the Nazi-held coast of Normandy took place on 6 June 1944, thousands of nurses, doctors, corpsmen, and supporting hospital staff had been waiting for

months in Great Britain to cross the English Channel with the troops.

In June of 1944, Nolan was to be shipped out across the Atlantic and stationed in England until her unit was called forward. She thought that they would all be sent out to the French coast together, but it soon dawned on her that postings all happened in fits and spurts.

A month later, she found herself on a fully packed ship headed for Utah Beach in Normandy, nervous as hell. It was a month after D-Day and she and 17 other combat nurses were ready to jump overboard and drag themselves to shore as there were no docking bays on the beachfront.

Surely, the water is shallow enough here, Nolan thinks to herself as she peers over the boat at the splashing waves below. *The shore isn't too far away, I can make it.*

She jumps in along with the other nurses but quickly finds herself barely able to locate the sandy bottom with her boots. She panics, flailing her arms and feeling pulled down. It's certainly not helping that her already heavy backpack is getting thoroughly waterlogged, weighing her down further.

Almost on the verge of losing breath and swallowing too much ocean water, she feels a sudden tug at her backpack and finds herself above water! Taking a huge breath, she looks up to see a fellow nurse, a good head taller than herself, helping her forward towards the beach.

Stunned and a little out of breath, Nolan looks around flabbergasted but happy to be on dry land in Europe... and alive, thanks to a little help from a Texan nurse blessed with some height.

The sergeants in charge told them all to hurry up and get moving off the beach as another unit was due to disembark soon. So they all gathered their things and began heading out to the next location on the beach to regroup and assess next steps.

This harried beach landing was the introduction to the most intensive year of Nolan's young adult life.

There...

"Where in God's name is all of our stuff?" Nolan asks her fellow nurses as they sit on the sand, wet, salty, and cold. Their supply truck, carrying all their hospital equipment, was supposed to be a couple of days behind them, and they needed to get moving to their next location soon. But without supplies?

Thank goodness it was still summer in Europe because the unit had no other option but to set up a temporary camp off the beachfront and wait. And wait they did. They set up the small "pup tents" that only housed two nurses and had barely enough space to sleep, never mind space for bathing and getting dressed.

A month later, after keeping themselves busy with neighboring field hospitals and soft training, their transport and core equipment (including bigger tents) finally arrived. The nurses never found out why they were so late, but that was just something they would become used to as the war raged around them.

Keep going and don't overthink. Without knowing it then, this would become the mantra of many WWII nurses.

Into The Thick of It

The 53rd FH was assigned to follow the Third Armored Division under the command of General George Patton; they headed up to Northern France. The field hospitals were usually meant to remain a good five miles behind the troops, but that guideline was not always adhered to.

When they arrived, the unit had only four hours to find a safe location and set up camp before ambulances and stretcher-bearers (two or four men who carried the wounded on stretchers) arrived with soldiers from the front. Sometimes the wounded would arrive before the hospital was fully set up and cots would have to be quickly stationed according to how the patients arrived. In an interview with The American Legion in 2014, Nolan noted: "It wasn't quite the way they had instructed us to do it, but you know, you improvise a lot."

Although their heavy casualty field hospital unit often looked like a jumbled mess of commands and scrambling people to the untrained eye, they were, in fact, one of the best units at the time. They would keep pace and take care of hundreds of men working seamlessly within the well-organized system called the

Chain of Evacuation—the process of receiving, treating, operating on, and stabilizing the critically wounded (non-transportables) before they would be sent off to the Evacuation Hospital (EH) closer to safety.

Nolan and the other sisters in the casualty ward had one critical criterion for patient survival: To treat them within "The Golden Hour." This was the 60 minutes they needed to get the patient from a state of shock into a stabilized state (stable vitals and controlled bleeding). If it took longer than an hour, the patient was likely not going to make it. This term, coined by Nolan herself, would later be used throughout the medical community.

In her 2021 book, *The Girls Who Stepped Out of Line: Untold Stories of the Women Who Changed the Course of World War II*, Mari K. Eder divulges a snippet from an interview with Nolan describing the state of the FHs: "Sometimes the boom of artillery was too close for comfort. IV poles rattled, and medicines shook off the shelves and onto the dirt floors of the tents. Wounded soldiers moaned in their sleep."

Luckily for her, their unit was never bombed directly, but they often felt the shudder and confusion from being in such close proximity to the actual fighting. To subdue the terrified and shellshocked men, the nurses would often pull them out of their cots and lay with them on the ground, holding them tight to ease the trembling until the action had dissipated.

Months passed, and the coldest weather in 40 years hit Europe that winter. Nolan remembers how freezing cold it was: "The first enemy was fighting the weather" (American Legion HQ, 2014). They had to work through blizzards, deep snow, and constant frost, which directly impacted their own health and all their equipment.

Keeping the patients warm was of the highest priority as Nolan and the other nurses kept potbelly stoves running throughout the day and night in the wards and swaddled the men like babies in as many blankets as they could find. The cold was relentless and unforgiving.

A partial favor to their climate battle was the fact that they were always moving. Being stationary for too long would remind them of how cold and miserable they really were. But since they were in constant motion—packing, repacking, unpacking, and treating patients—they were on their feet all the time. The coldest they felt was when they were in their own cots trying to catch a couple of hours of shut-eye before the next shift.

At this stage of events in the European theater of war, we find Katherine Nolan and her unit at the Battle of the Bulge. This was the German army's final effort in December of 1944 to invade further west into Belgium, France, and Luxemburg in an attempt to surprise attack the Allied forces there. The Battle of the Bulge was named so because of the shape German frontline troops made when drawn on military maps as they pushed quickly westwards.

Nolan found herself in the center of the action, as that year her division was in Holland, heading ever closer to the German border. Years later, Nolan wrote an article in the *Bulge Bugle* (a journal for the veterans of the Bulge) about her experience during those frost-ridden two months in Holland. She begins with the explanation of how she and her unit would often huddle at the back of their transport truck for warmth and often found locals staring at them as they walked by.

Imagine these once rather sophisticated women now reduced to rattling bones under khaki blankets huddling together against the cruel wind and waiting for the rest of the convoy so they could set up tents. She writes (Stamberg, 2004):

> We had K-rations all day. Cold, tasteless cans… something that was called scrambled eggs and meat, those dog biscuits they called crackers. Some powder to mix with water in the mess kit tin cup. Lemonade it was called. Meanwhile, the temperature kept dropping and it looked like snow. The tarp covering the top of the truck gave a little protection from the wind but that was all. We were dirty, weary, and chilled to the point of numbness. (para. 10)

By the grace of all things good, she relates, someone finally found a school nearby that was willing to let them use it as a hospital base for a couple of weeks. They eagerly accepted; it would be the first building they lived in since landing on Utah beach.

The premises proved to be perfect for hospital setup. They had just finished preparing all the equipment when the first lot of casualties arrived after having encountered German troops nearby. The unit worked for 14 hours straight trying to stabilize and assess the situation.

Unexpected Merriment

A couple of days later, when things seemed to have calmed down ever so slightly, Nolan recalls seeing nuns enter the makeshift hospital and look around curiously. There was a church not too far up the road, and the priest was the person who permitted the unit to move into the school. She writes amusingly (Stamberg, 2004):

> They were surprised to see us nursing patients. They, like the villagers, had taken the six of us for prostitutes since we wore the same uniforms as the male officers, including the pants, and these were what the camp followers wore. (para. 13)

After some much-needed explanation, thanks to the Dutch translation between the priest (who spoke very little English) and the nuns, the godly women offered the nurses to stay with them in the convent down the road where they had clean beds and hot baths to share. *Well! This must be Christmas!* Nolan thought to herself. Of course, they would take up that offer!

The script of a 2004 NPR interview with Susan Stamberg gives us insight into their lodging in the convent:

> Six of their beds were ready for our use. The nuns and twenty-eight war orphans in their care slept in the basement. They at first expected us to join them there, but at this point, we were

ready to die in our beds if need be in comfort. To sleep in a real bed under a roof was such luxury that we felt spoiled and pampered. (para. 17)

The closer it came to Christmas, the more the unit expected to get a call to move on after treating the 84th Division. But that call never came. Something altogether beautiful happened in the week leading up to the 25th. Everyone relaxed and got into the Christmas spirit as much as the situation allowed.

Small pine trees were chopped down, brought into the wards, and decorated with tin can cutouts of stars and bandages hung to look like tinsel. Men were smiling and happy, singing songs to the sound of the school organ played by a young local, while eating loads of Life Savers candy that the Red Cross had supplied in cartons, and eating hastily baked cakes made by the service cook, thanks to the flour and sugar graciously supplied by the nuns.

But on December 23rd, they received the news to start evacuating and dismantling the hospital. This did not break the patients' spirits, as jovial laughter was still heard between nurse and patient while they prepared themselves for the cold trip to the General Hospital nearby.

On Christmas Eve, a small mass was held in the chapel where all the staff and locals congregated. Once the mass was over, they sat down to an elaborate table setting and a delicious meal. They conversed with the Dutch nuns as best they could, using hand gestures and signals. They roughly understood each other and seemed to enjoy each other's company. But as the final tea was being served, the nurses heard the unmistakable sound of idle truck engines outside.

"Report at once. It's time to leave," said the driver who had abruptly burst into the dining room of the convent.

"Please tell the colonel to give us five more minutes," replied the chief nurse, Marie, understanding that her charges just wanted to drink their tea and say goodbye.

"Yes ma'am," said the officer and awkwardly left the room.

Nolan remembered those five minutes being the longest five minutes of her life. One reason was that the tea was boiling hot, and the other was the long stares they shared, the kind smiles of gratitude, and the trickle of tears as they contemplated their goodbyes.

Soon, the horns were tooting, and that was the final warning they needed to get going. Keeping up with the convoy was no small feat! Nolan heard a male officer loudly proclaim to his friend as they boarded the back of the truck, "Those damn women are holding up the war" (Stamberg, 2004).

Off they went, further up into the heart of the Third Reich. She and the 53rd FH, followed their platoon into a deadly arena, a Christmas Day she would never forget.

The war was coming to an end. Nolan didn't know this yet, but it would be the last direct combat that the European theater would see. The Battle of the Bulge was a month to remember, and by January of the following year, 1945, Allied armies would eventually overwhelm the German troops, causing retreat and Allied victory.

During this time, Nolan not only treated her own Allied troops, but also the German POWs that were required to get the same level of care before being released.

What was truly remarkable about Nolan's year in Europe with her unit was that they had traversed five different countries and experienced the most battle-intensive areas of the entire war, more so than the majority of Allied troops out there! From Normandy into Northern France, then Central Europe, and through the Ardennes into the Rhineland of Germany, the 53rd FH kept up their good work, saving hundreds, if not thousands of lives.

In May of 1945, the announcement of the Victory in Europe (VE Day) arrived while Nolan was working in the German Hospital in Kirn, near Frankfurt, treating all kinds of patients. Due to her marvelous and honorable work, she and other nurses within her unit were elevated to the rank of First Lieutenant.

For three months they remained in Germany awaiting news of the war in Japan. During this time, the 53rd FH treated survivors of the Nazi concentration camps and released American POWs. Once the European field had been "stabilized," the unit was positioned to embark for the Japanese island and continue the work there. Luckily enough, that plan was nullified as the Japanese officially surrendered that August.

It was time to go home.

... And Back Again

"I do," she says while smiling up at John. It's 1946 and Katherine Flynn is now Katherine Nolan.

They were married rather quickly after they had both returned to the US. Of course, it was meant to be. The Air Force Lieutenant Colonel John Nolan fell in love with Katherine years prior and was not going to let this opportunity pass him by.

From there on, Nolan started living the life of a typical 26-year-old. She would have six children with John, many of whom would later enlist in the army themselves, fighting in Vietnam, Afghanistan, and Iraq.

Her family members are lovers of poetry. Nolan's granddaughter, Nooriel, at the age of 14 wrote a poem for her granny titled "Nana Kate." A few haunting verses of the poem read (Stamberg, 2004):

> The screams...
>
> from soldiers echo in her ears.
>
> She sleeps on a cot,
>
> when she sleeps at all,
>
> uses her helmet like a sink
>
> to wash her hair.
>
> It doesn't show her
>
> bloodstained hands...

or the pain she feels

for the men needing them.

How accurately Nooriel depicts her grandmother's
struggles with self-doubt and her weariness of the war
conditions. Her mature writing shows that a surreal
sense of tragedy was passed on from grandma to
grandchild. It is no wonder that Nolan's visit to Utah
Beach in 2001, as the only female in a group of
veterans, triggered flashbacks of their landing years
earlier. She was subsequently diagnosed with PTSD.

Her husband, John, passed away in 2005, after a 60-year
marriage together in Naples, Florida.

One of the many frustrations for frontline nurses was
the rapid turnover of their patients and the lack of
follow-up. At a Battle of the Bulge veterans' reunion,
she was recognized by a former soldier who told her
that she had saved his life. This was a tremendous high
point for Nolan, who said, "I felt like I waited all my
life to meet just one of my former patients and know
that he made it all the way home" (Stamberg, 2004).

In 2007, Nolan received the award of the highest
French order of merit known as The Legion of Honor.
She was the only female to receive it that day in France.
She also became an avid member of the Veterans of the
Battle of the Bulge and a member of the Women in
Military Service for America (WIMSA), as well as a
member of the Reserves Officers Association (ROA).

In March of 2019, Katherine Flynn Nolan passed
away at the age of 98 in Florida, leaving behind her 6

children, 14 grandchildren, and 10 great-grandchildren. What a beautiful brood to be survived by!

Whether we criticize the fact that it took over 30 years for her contributions to be acknowledged, or marvel at the fact that she miraculously survived a tour of duty from which many others never returned home, what we can say with great confidence is that this nurse, who did so much in such a short period of time, left a legacy which remains an inspiration to many women.

Chapter 2:

Marcella LeBeau

The life she has known is about to change. She doesn't really know if it is for good or for bad, but she knows that she will be a part of something big.

Yes, the color of her skin and the language she speaks are different from the majority on this ship, yet she is an American citizen, and she has a right to defend her country in any way she can.

This is her mantra as she lies in the sleeping quarters of the ship along with hundreds of other qualified nurses like herself. They are packed like sardines, and they are going into a situation that most people have never encountered before. The conditions of warfare are so obviously cruel that the excitement of travel is shrouded by the sadness of the circumstances.

The commanding officer was blunt in his preparation for their trip. We can imagine his speech to the crew: "Be brave, men and women of America. We are traversing the Atlantic. This is no pleasure cruise; this is no holiday. The only way we can serve is to arrive alive and do our duty for the country. And with that in mind, listen to your orders, commence drills as instructed, and pray."

Indeed, she would pray and serve others for as long as her life would ensure.

The Venture

Her father, John. M Ryan, was an American with Irish heritage, and her mother, Florence (Four Bear), was a native of the Lakota tribe. Her parents' lives read something like a Pocahontas story.

Her father had great respect for the Lakota people, and he often conveyed that to Marcella and her four siblings when they were young. He believed that "the Native people are the greatest people on earth" although Marcella recalls that "he couldn't say the same for his own" (*Marcella LeBeau*, 2021).

Her Lakota name *Wigmuke Waste' Win* (Pretty Rainbow Woman) was passed on from her grandmother, Louise Bare Face, after her own mother had passed when she was just 10 years old. LeBeau held this name with pride for the rest of her life as a symbol of her heritage.

Her heritage was indeed important; one of her descendants fought in the horrifying Battle of Little Bighorn (the Natives defeating the US troops) while the other reluctantly signed the infamous Fort Laramie Treaty of 1868, forcing Natives to move further west onto predetermined reservations.

At the beginning of the 20th century, relations were still fragile between the Native American people and the Colonial invaders; Native people still resented the White people for being mistreated and systematically killed off. It had been over 400 years since the English arrived in their "New World," and now they were imposing their own rules and setting boundaries for people who had lived on this land for thousands of years before.

Native Americans were segregated, just as African Americans were in the Segregation Era in the United States between 1900 and 1939. In repeated attempts to eradicate their culture, Native Americans were forced from their lands and given smaller pieces of land on which to settle. They faced an impossible choice. If Native American individuals chose to remove themselves from their community and live a "solitary and normalized Western lifestyle," then they were allowed to take American citizenship. If they refused and decided to remain in their tiny, segregated communities, then that citizenship was denied.

LeBeau grew up in this time of hardship and was never permitted to speak her native Lakota language in front of anyone else in her boarding school. Children who didn't follow these rules were punished. The mistreatment she faced as a half-Native American girl in the segregated "Indian" boarding school was equal to those who held full Native blood.

As the eldest, with her father often away for work, she had the responsibility of caring for her brothers and sister, cooking, and cleaning, whilst still studying in school. John Ryan was a good father who brought up his four children (the youngest, Leo, passed soon after his mother) to the best of his abilities and often instilled a sense of "education first" saying, "Go get a good education because no one can take that away from you" (*Marcella LeBeau*, 2021), LeBeau would recall fondly.

And so she did just that.

For Others

LeBeau had taken care of her ill mother when she was younger, then her younger siblings, and then her father, so she knew where her passions lay. She understood from a young age what good it did for her to do good for others.

She went into her three-year nursing program at St. Mary's Hospital in the nearby town of Pierre in South Dakota where she earned her undergraduate degree in 1942 at the age of 23. At St. Mary's she received extensive surgical ward training and was greatly helped by the surgeon in charge, Dr. Riggs.

LeBeau (then Ryan) was busying herself after the lesson with Dr. Riggs, where all the training nurses would stand around him while he illustrated equipment, observing and taking notes. That day he called her aside and said, "Miss Ryan, I believe?"

"Yes, sir," she replied apprehensively, not knowing what she might have done wrong.

"I read in your file that you are from the Sioux Reservation. I happen to speak Lakota and have always found greatness in your culture." He proceeded with "*Hau*," and holding up his hand in greeting, "*Tókheškhe yaúŋ he?*"

LeBeau was astounded to find him asking casually how she was doing in her own tongue. It was maybe a little rough in the intonation, but lovely to hear.

"*Wašté*," she quickly replied smoothly and with a huge smile on her face.

Yes, she was good and happy to find someone on her side who saw past her skin color. She recalled how she enjoyed his lessons as he was a very skilled teacher, always encouraging LeBeau to speak her Native tongue whenever possible and to be proud.

After graduating as an RN, she worked for a little while at St. Thomas Hospital. She and her friend Marie were egged on by another doctor into experiencing a little more than just their corner of the world. He said to them one day, "You girls are young, you have an education. Why don't you go out and see the world?"

True. Why not? The wider world was beckoning.

So they both decided to join a GH in Pontiac, Michigan through a job advertisement in a nursing magazine. Both of the women were accepted and each paid $174 a month, including meals and boarding, which was a great deal back then.

The 1943 war news was booming over the radio, promoting and requesting nurses join the military. LeBeau and Marie quickly enlisted in the Army Nurses Corps (ANC) so they could take their skills to more people.

She had completed her month's military training in California and was posted at a temporary opening in a psychiatric hospital until she received a call to travel to Boston, Massachusetts for assignment duty overseas.

The time had come. She signed her papers, collected her uniform, and boarded the *USS George Washington* headed for England that fall of 1943. She was 24, inexperienced, and green around the gills with seasickness, but that didn't matter since this was just one leg of the bigger adventure to come.

There...

Marcella LeBeau took her first step on foreign soil in Liverpool, England, just having endured the worst two weeks of sleep in her life on a ship that carried 5,000 other troops and nurses. She had no idea how much worse it was going to get.

From Liverpool, she boarded a truck headed to Wales. Once there, she waited for her call. Her unit was drilled in basic army conduct and operations to prepare for being called further into Europe to assist Allied troops. "Hurry up and wait" was the name of the game. Just like Kate Nolan in the previous chapter, LeBeau expected to dive into action, but all she seemed to do was wait.

The town in which they were situated was in rough shape and still under constant attack, so everything had to be boarded up and blacked out. LeBeau recalls having to walk over rubble from bombed-out buildings everywhere she went, shining her torch downwards in case enemy aircraft spotted the light. And this was only a first taste of what was to come.

As it turned out, she was not posted at the front just yet, but instead commissioned to the 76th GH unit in Leominster, in the West Midlands, where she served as a psychiatric nurse in their wards for a couple of months preparing for D-Day.

A Dangerous Homefront

"Some of them [soldiers] couldn't see, some of them couldn't hear. So we gave them sodium amytal narcosis" (American Veterans Center, 2020), says LeBeau, recalling how the sedative would bring the patients into a deep unconsciousness allowing the nurses and doctors to treat and manage the patient safely.

LeBeau enjoyed the job, but her true calling was in the surgical wards where she had trained, so she was always on the lookout for a post in that facet of nursing. Then she got the call she was looking for. The request to work in her preferred ward was accepted just as the first wave of injured soldiers arrived from the beaches of D-Day.

Quick history lesson: D-Day (Operation Overlord) occurred in June 1944 and was the largest seaborne invasion in recorded history. The American, British, and Canadian troops flooded the Normandy beach and entered the European theater with a bang. The German leaders were bamboozled by the false information fed by Allied intelligence that led them to believe they would be invaded further south, which allowed the Allies to enter and dominate the unsuspecting German skeleton army in that region.

Because LeBeau was in a GH, they were usually stationed in semi-permanent locations within and around major cities which had electricity and running water (*The Army Nurse Corps*, 2014):

Nurses were sent to ready Station and General Hospitals in preparation for a new offensive often moved into abandoned, bombed-out hospitals, schools, or factories and became scrubwomen and scavengers in a hurried attempt to prepare for the expected inundation of battle casualties. (para. 53)

Within the Chain of Evacuation, the GHs were the last line for the allied soldier. If he arrived at a GH, then he was sure to make it home, as by now he had passed from all the other temporary units and stations where he was examined by many different nurses and doctors, before finally lying down under an actual roof.

Some of the soldiers were reclassified and sent out to duty again, and others were shipped back to the United States. "Both station and general hospitals also accepted patients from outside the chain of evacuation, such as servicemen and women who needed treatment for pneumonia or various contagious diseases" (*The Army Nurse Corps*, 2014).

It is important to note that even though Station Hospitals (SH) and General Hospitals (GH) were further from the enemy line than FH or EH hospitals, they were still under fire from air raids by the German and Japanese Air Force. When the action had calmed down a little bit, LeBeau and her unit would be sent down to Southampton beach to wait for a Dutch ship to take them over the English Channel into Normandy.

Battling the Front Line

LeBeau arrived at Utah beach on the Normandy coast in late August of that year after three horrible days of travel in choppy waters. Unlike our previous heroine, LeBeau had an easier time disembarking, as her landing barge dropped its bow right on the beach.

The FH and EH units were so well equipped that they sometimes rivaled National Hospitals at home. They had the newest equipment, the best medication, and the best staff possible. In fact, this was one of the top reasons that nurses and doctors joined the military service in WWII. A huge amount of funding went into healthcare over those six years, and anyone with an ounce of ambition could see that military medical service was a great challenge and career boost.

LeBeau's unit had been waiting for several weeks for their trucks and equipment to arrive, with senior officers continuously reminding the nurses not to stroll around the field as there were landmines around! Fortunately, they could still visit the area; some of the nurses would get the opportunity to pick out of a hat and go out on excursions to nearby towns.

One night, LeBeau was invited to a small banquet hosted by a French lady who wept while singing the French national anthem at the dinner, making the whole group emotional. The people living in countries occupied by Axis forces suffered tremendously over the loss of their rights and freedoms. Imagine what that must have meant for the Allied nurses and doctors who could do nothing more than watch in sympathetic silence.

When the equipment and transport did eventually arrive, the unit was taken up to the Beaujon GH in Paris that had previously been in the hands of the Germans before the Americans took over. The first thing LeBeau saw when she arrived was a huge Nazi flag bearing a swastika on the front of the building, which was rapidly torn down.

LeBeau worked tirelessly in the surgical ward within the 108th GH, but not without the few nights scattered here and there when the women were able to go see a typical French cabaret at the Folies Bergère and ascend the Eiffel Tower (not all the way to the top, of course, because it was dangerous with all the buzz bombs). The staff took every opportunity that came up to enjoy themselves, as a much-needed release of psychological stress.

From Paris, the unit had moved up to a GH in Liège, Belgium, to join their original 76th GH. Over those months between 1944 and 1945, the unit took care of patients who had fought in the Battle of the Bulge. The hospital received over 89,000 American casualties.

LeBeau's ward was the A1 surgical ward, which saw the incoming patients in need of amputations, severe wound surgery, and blood transfusions. But other casualty wards addressed foot rot, disease, frostbite, and concussions. LeBeau mentioned (American Veterans Center, 2020):

We had buzz bombs day and night in Liège and the patients there had divided the sky into three areas. The middle area was what they called "buzz bomb alley"' so when they hollered *buzz bomb* at you then you were supposed to take cover.

In early January of 1945, LeBeau was just about to get off night duty in the shock ward at the Belgian GH when she heard a scream. She had been cowering down all evening from the shockwaves of buzz bombs hitting buildings in their vicinity, but she didn't think they had touched her unit.

A nurse approached her just as she was about to go to her quarters to clean up and get some sleep. The nurse was sobbing profusely saying, "Don't go there. It's awful! There are limbs all over" (American Veterans Center, 2020).

A buzz bomb had struck and destroyed the officer's station in the hospital, which was filled with men getting ready for bed. A total of 25 officers were killed.

The nurse finally said, after calming herself down, "They'll need you tonight. So go back and get some sleep, because they'll need you tonight."

"I'm so glad I never saw that," mentions LeBeau in her interview (American Veterans Center, 2020). She might not have needed to see the macabre sight, but someone else had to identify those 25 men. She would meet him years later.

He recounted how one of the men was unidentifiable, and thus sectioned as Missing in Action (MIA). Later, they found a single hand, preserved and lifeless, with a wedding ring on one of the fingers. The man knew that ring. He knew to whom it belonged, and from there, was able to identify his deceased friend.

What's fascinating about these countless stories from medical staff was their pure ignorance of what was actually happening outside the hospital. For good reason, these nurses and doctors were focused on the casualties of the war, not on the war itself. They did not know who was winning and who was losing; they simply didn't have the time to inquire or ascertain the truth about the information they did receive.

Many medical staff only found out about the battles that were waged and the reasons behind them much later. LeBeau and the other hospital staff, for example, didn't know that their hospital was literally sitting between the oncoming German troops and the retreating Americans. Official channels only provided need-to-know information: When to start dismantling and getting ready for immediate evacuation to the next site.

They could see the sky light up the night as if it were day, filled with flares and bombs. They could hear the trucks roaring down the main road in town, and they could feel the intense vibrations from the ground activity outside. The Liège river reflecting the destruction above looked as if it were itself on fire.

She recalled, "It was wartime and things were fast-moving." Patients moved through quickly, but she said of one overnight case: "I just can't forget that look. The skin stretched over his bones and that vacant stare... And he wouldn't talk. It's embedded in my memory" (American Veterans Center, 2020).

By the time January had come and gone, and the world was waiting in anticipation for the surrender of Japan, LeBeau was still attending to the influx of men from the field.

"Marcella," cried out a man lying beside LeBeau's desk in the surgical ward reception.

"Yes," she replied in slight irritation. *How does this man know my first name?* she wondered.

"Remember me, Willie, from school?" he said with wide eyes and hopeful cheer.

"Willie?" *Yes.* She remembered a young boy, short as grass with a pleasant face from the early days in South Dakota. And there he lay, just waiting to be sent back home.

A small world offered up a small but amazing co-incidence.

Like Nolan, LeBeau stated that one of the greatest honors of her service was a reunion with her former patient. Eugene Roubideaux was a Native American soldier and double amputee, who had been brought into the shock ward in Liege, where LeBeau was on night duty. LeBeau stayed by his bedside to encourage him as much as she could, as he was thought to be a suicide risk. After a 40-year search, LeBeau had an emotional reunion with him. He had become a role model for other veteran amputees. A success story to make any front line nurse proud, knowing she had played a part in restoring him to life.

... And Back Again

LeBeau walked into a drug store in the center of town to purchase some rubbing alcohol for cleaning at home. Having returned to her hometown in South Dakota, seeing her siblings and family was wonderful after those crazy years. Yet some things really had not changed.

"Yes ma'am. What can I do for you?" the pharmacist asks pleasantly from behind the counter.

"Some rubbing alcohol, please. Two bottles should be fine, thank you," she replies easily.

The stare she received from the pharmacist alerted her that something was off. "Sorry, ma'am. We cannot sell that to you."

Other times she would get the excuse, "Oh, no, we are out of stock."

A policy had been implemented by the American government prohibiting the sale of alcohol, including over-the-counter drugs that contained it, to Native Americans who resided on the Reservations.

This severe bias towards Natives was later changed in the 1950s, although for all those years prior, LeBeau was never able to buy from the pharmacy herself, but had to ask White acquaintances to buy something as ordinary as rubbing alcohol for her. This was a sure sign that she still had a lot of work to do here at home. Perceptions had to change.

LeBeau was discharged as First Lieutenant when she retired from the army in 1946 and she remembers how "in all the time I was in the military, I never once experienced discrimination. Never once" (American Veterans Center, 2020). "I think they accepted me for my ability as a surgical nurse," LeBeau says to her interviewer. "Exactly how it should be," he replies (American Veterans Center, 2020). Yet she came home to ostracization and disrespect.

In 1947, Marcella Rose Ryan tied the knot with Gilbert LeBeau and proceeded to have eight children.

Marcella Rose LeBeau did not end her career in helping others when the world had stopped fighting itself. Over the next 30 years, she dedicated her life to another cause—caring for and honoring her people and their progress in society. She worked as a nurse on the Cheyenne Reservation, where she also stood on the Tribal Council from 1990 to 1994, advocating for many rights in their communities and making critical policy decisions.

Years later, LeBeau and her daughter Kathy returned to Liège in Belgium to find the plaque for those 25 men who died in her hospital that night in 1945. She finally found a woman who knew where the plaque was located. The woman took LeBeau and her daughter to the Henri-Chapelle American Cemetery and Memorial, where LeBeau was finally able to read the names on that plaque and recognize their sacrifice.

The previously bombed Liège hospital had eventually become a transportation company. When LeBeau and other veterans notified the company of the disaster that occurred there, the leadership chose to build a section of their garden into a memorial site and moved the plaque from the cemetery to its appropriate location to honor the fallen.

Among the many awards LeBeau received from her war service was the European-African-Middle Eastern Campaign Medal due to her incredible involvement in several WWII campaigns.

LeBeau also received her French Legion of Honor award in 2004, a good 58 years after she returned from duty. Two years after that, she was honored in the South Dakota Hall of Fame for a lifetime of work in the state and for its people. In 2016, the 97-year-old was awarded the Women in History Award and an honorary doctorate degree in 2018 from South Dakota State University.

Finally, in November of 2021, LeBeau was inducted into the National Native Hall of Fame. The 102-year-old woman was humbled, accepting with "The greatest honor that I can receive is from my own people. And I am here tonight being honored by my own people" (*Marcella LeBeau*, 2021).

She passed away in the Cheyenne River hospital a few weeks later, survived by her many daughters and her last living son, including all the grandchildren, great-grandchildren, and great-great-grandchildren.

This matriarch, prolific nurse, and advocate for women and her Native American community would leave behind a legacy that called for unity and the abolition of discrimination. She showed the world that women, no matter their origin, could lead a life of courage and determination by taking advantage of opportunities given and by creating their own. LeBeau was a beautiful woman who inspired others to do better with the little time (or a long time, in her case) that we get in this life.

The British QAs

& Australian AANS

The next two stories cross the oceans to the theater of war in the Far East and the part played by nurses from Great Britain and Australia in WWII.

The British QAs

"Wherever the Army goes, the QAs go. In military hospitals their grey dresses and short scarlet capes - surely a most beautiful nursing uniform - meant a cessation from pain to every ailing serviceman" (Bowden & Barclay, 2015).

QA is an acronym for Queen Alexandra. The QAs encompassed nurses from Great Britain and the British Commonwealth countries of Australia and New Zealand. The "touch of scarlet" became symbolic of hope to many wounded soldiers in the care of a QA nurse.

Florence Nightingale was pivotal in the development of the nursing profession, and she is still honored today. Her work in the Crimean War of 1854 was the first recognition of nursing service for the army. She fought for the employment of women nurses in military hospitals and established an Army Training School for military nurses. In 1881, the military nursing was called the Army Nursing Service, then in 1897, the Princess Christians Army Nursing Service Reserve (PCANSR) was created to assist in the First Boer War in South Africa.

By 1902, the PCANSR established the name of Queen Alexandra's Imperial Military Nursing Service (QAIMNS) through the Royal Warrant. Queen Alexandra (married to King Edward VII) became president and instilled her Danish heritage through the Order of Dannebrog. The image below shows the QAIMNS badge on the left of the nurse's tippet and the insignia of the Order of Dannebrog on the right.

In 1947, the QAIMNS were enveloped by the British Army and renamed Queen Alexandra's Royal Army Nursing Corps (QARANC), informally known as the QAs.

Male nurses were only allowed to join the QAs after 1992 when they were transferred from the Royal Army Medical Corps (RAMC) and incorporated into the QA units. Male nursing students and orderlies still worked under QAs, although they could only qualify and enlist within the RAMC (not QAIMNS) during WWII.

QAs were the first to arrive in Europe and tend to soldiers in 1939 when the Germans invaded France. This period came to be known as the "Phoney War," as little fighting actually occurred during that time. That period ended in 1940 when the QAs had to quickly retreat under heavy German attack.

The evacuation of British troops, after the 6-week battle of France ended in France's surrender, was codenamed Operation Dynamo but is more widely known as Dunkirk.

QAs returned later in the war and were some of the last to leave the European theater after the occurrences of D-Day. From the initial 600 original members, the department grew to 12,000 due to their large efforts overseas.

Rank

The hierarchy within the QAs was highly regarded for three main reasons. First, it was the first time ever that women were granted a rank designation alongside their male counterparts. Second, it took years of service to get promoted, so rank was not bestowed lightly. Third, rank could be used as leverage for recognition and remuneration.

As of 1941, their initial ranking started with the Staff Nurse (without rank), then Sister (Lieutenant), Senior Sister (Captain), Matron (Major), followed by Principal Matron (Lieutenant-Colonel), then Chief Principal Matron (Colonel), and finally, the highest rank of Matron in Chief (Brigadier).

Below the rank of Staff Nurse or even Lieutenant, you would find the orderlies. These were usually young men responsible for cleaning and monitoring patients, keeping records, and assisting the Sister in her more robust daily duties. The orderly would train and be supervised by the Sister and sometimes be sent out as field medics on the battlefield. These men initially earned more than the qualified and experienced RNs, which quickly changed when the nurses requested an amendment to rank pay.

Above all the nurses and orderlies were the surgeons and doctors. While they didn't run the wards per se (that was left to the Chief nurse and her team), they scheduled patient assessments, operations, and checkups.

Medical supply and ward preparation was mainly conducted by the nurses and orderlies, but the doctors and physicians had the harder job, if you will, of deciding who would be sent back down the Chain of Evacuation and who would go back into the field to possibly "die again." For many of the doctors, WWII meant making the army your patient, rather than individual men, leaving the nurses to have the heart to get the men through.

Penicillin

It is important to note that the QAs were the first units to use penicillin on patients in France in WWII. This was a monumental and lucky discovery by the Scottish physician Alexander Fleming, just in time for the devastation and grime that was to come.

"QAs and medical offices were estimated to have saved up to 15% of lives with the new super drug penicillin" (*QA World War Two nursing*, n.d.), and would have to administer the drug every three hours. This was no easy task as they had to mix the yellow penicillin powder with a saline solution, while still maintaining utmost sterilization. This resulted in intensive preparation regimes for the administration rounds of penicillin in field and evacuation hospitals.

Australian AANS

That brings us to Great Britain's former colony, good ol' Australia, which became independent from the Empire in 1901 and controlled its own armed forces (what little they had) before WWII. Joining the war in the name of their old Empire was a bold and strategic maneuver as Great Britain would bring their extensive military forces into Australia. But waging war from the Australian front became a necessity when Japan invaded.

The typical Australian culture can be described as jovial and no-nonsense. That spirit became pivotal to their achievements in the war, especially those of the nurses. Equally as brilliant as their British Sisters, yet born and bred in a completely different environment, they brought their stamina and tough demeanor to the war's nursing efforts.

The Australian and Canadian Nurses would often try to prove themselves of equal caliber to their Sisters of the Empire in a sort of undisclosed competition between the nations.

The Australian forces worked in some of the roughest and harshest environments of the Middle East, North Africa, and Pacific regions, and also followed their countrymen in the Mediterranean as well as Great Britain.

The Australian Army Nurse Service (AANS) was established in 1902 as a reserve in national emergencies and staffed by civilian nurses who volunteered for duty at home and overseas. The AANS, along with the

Voluntary Aid Detachments (VAD), were the only service corps in which the women could enroll. The AANS remained active throughout WWI and WWII until 1949, when it was attained by the Australian Army, thus becoming the Royal Australian Army Nursing Corps (RAANC).

The AANS pledge of service read (Heywood, 2002):

> I pledge myself loyally to serve my King and Country and to maintain the honour and efficiency of the Australian Army Nursing Service.

> I will do all in my power to alleviate the suffering of the sick and wounded, sparing no effort to bring them comfort of body and peace of mind.

> I will work in unity and comradeship with my fellow nurses.

> I will be ready to give assistance to those in need of my help, and will abstain from any action which may bring sorrow and suffering to others.

> At all times I will endeavour to uphold the highest traditions of Womanhood and of the Profession of which I am Part.

Branching Out

The Australian Army and that of New Zealand would collectively come to be known as the Australian and

New Zealand Army Corps (ANZACS), aligning the RNs from each to enroll under the one banner.

Within the six years of WWII, 3,500 nurses enlisted and served worldwide, dividing into the two separate branches of the military—the Royal Australian Naval Nursing Service (RANNS) and the Royal Australian Air Force Nursing Service (RAAFNS).

The concern for most of the Allied governments within the initial years of war was not staffing enough capable nurses, but staffing enough capable *military* nurses. As explained earlier, these women needed to know bedside care and general nursing as well as combat lingo, division codes, mapping, and military routines to be able to keep up with the Australian and British fighting divisions over the battlefields.

Like all the other Allied nurse corps around the world, Australia revised their uniforms. At the beginning of the war, nurses were sent out to the heat, mud and blood of the battlefields in their white robes, starched collars and veils. This quickly turned out to be very impractical; thus in 1942, most of the field, evacuation, and station hospitals were staffed by women dressed in khaki pants and shirts, or with far more practical drab brown dresses and caps suited for outdoor work.

And some interesting outdoor work they did.

Medivacs

It became very clear to Allied leaders that WWII covered greater distances than its predecessor, and that the use of airplanes in the evacuation was a rapid means to retrieve injured troops. So along with the Royal Australian Air Force (RAAF), the government formed the Air Ambulance Units (AAU) and Medical Air Evacuation Transport Units (MAETU).

Expanding the medical evacuation (medivac) units was a necessity due to the sheer number of casualties. Therefore by 1944, the Australian government created the Royal Australian Air Force Nursing Service (RAAFNS) to train the nurses who would board large evacuation planes (some could hold up to 18 stretchers) and head straight into enemy territory to retrieve soldiers.

These specialized units sped up the Chain of Evacuation and were able to run in coastal regions and pacific islands, thanks to the use of flying boats. The nurses onboard these planes were known as the Flying Angels and specialized in inflight care, tropical hygiene, and general survival and emergency procedures.

It is noteworthy to mention that women flew the planes too. The Allied nations, out of solutions and desperate for staff, developed the first female units in their respective Air Forces. In Australia, the Women's Auxiliary Australian Air Force (WAAAF) was established, with female pilots delivering supplies to base camps or ferrying aircraft back home.

POWs

The most common affliction both British and Australian women of war faced was imprisonment and mistreatment by the Japanese soldiers in their occupation of Hong Kong and Singapore. Many QA and AANS nurses found themselves keeping company with other Prisoners of War (POW).

The modesty of these women is astounding. In typical fashion, their acts of bravery were often downplayed, as described in the war journal of an Australian nurse, Joyce Ffoulkes Parry, who faced the war in her own turbulent way. Parry writes (2015):

> If by some chance I should become a war victim too, and who can tell who may or may not be - I should hate to think my name was inscribed on a brass roll of honor - as though I were some heroine - which emphatically I am not and should be perfectly happy knowing I had done my job according to my own standards. (p. 86)

The stories of the British and Australian nurses of WWII are a life lesson on courage and the will to survive; when all else seems lost, hope still remains.

Chapter 3:

Margot Turner

Years have passed since she last ate a decent meal. She can hardly remember the flavor of the familiar comfort food of her childhood... a Sunday roast dinner, bread and butter pudding with custard, and oh, what wouldn't she have given for a nice pot of tea!

She looks down at herself miserably. She was once a gorgeous young woman —strong, vivacious, alive with life and love. Now she is a bag of bones, covered in rags, and filthy beyond comparison—not that she needs to compare herself to anyone in this prison.

Her crime: Being in the wrong place at the wrong time. A terrible piece of bad luck.

Propping herself up with difficulty to stand, she walks over to the cell door, which was not actually locked, and places her hands on the cold metal bars. She looks out over the prison courtyard, straining her eyes to see someone she recognizes.

Will I ever get out of here? I wonder how the other girls are doing. Are they still alive? Are they thinking about me?

These anxious questions are always at the forefront of her mind. Recently, her ruminations have started spiraling into hopelessness and despair. She must not lose hope! It's the only thing these men have not taken from her by force.

She was alive, and she must not forget that crucial fact meant she could still do some good, thanks to her training. She must keep her head down, her mouth shut, and keep praying that she makes it out before her body gives in.

Suddenly, a Japanese guard walks past her cell, bangs on the bars with his baton, and frightens her back into reality. He stares at her with contempt, barks with laughter and moves on to terrorize someone else.

The Venture

Eveline Marguerite Turner was born in 1910 in the North London suburb of Finchley.

She was the only girl of four siblings, with two older brothers, Dudley and Trevor, and one younger named Peter. Her mother, Molly Cecelia, and her father, Thomas Fredrick Turner, were good parents. She described her life as happy while she attended Finchley County School; the politics of war didn't affect her childhood much. Her father passed away when she was just 13 years of age, and her mother later remarried a gentleman named Ralph Saw.

There was general economic dismay in Great Britain and the rest of the world after WWI, with hunger strikes, epidemics, and unemployment on the rise. The Great Depression was kicking in. World wars were expensive and resource-hungry, which left many previously economically stable countries in absolute crisis. It would take a good 10 years for the economies of these once prosperous nations to recover, only then to be plunged back into a new war soon after.

During that time, Turner was just starting to get to know herself and what she wanted to do. "Picture a tall athletic young woman with wavy hair and bright blue eyes who excelled in swimming, tennis, and hockey and you see Margot Turner" (*QARANC*, 2021).

From a relatively early age, she knew that nursing was her calling. WWI and the influenza pandemic in 1918 had already left an undeniable mark on her immediate relatives, and she was sure that helping others would elevate her faith in God and align perfectly with her vision of modesty and strength.

She molded herself around her driving principles and "she studiously read the Bible, hoping to gain some divine perspective on the issues of life and death, and immersed herself in long periods of quiet introspection and prayer" (Starns, 2010). She also loved the outdoors and resented the idea of working behind a desk all her life.

Turner happened to be friends with older girls, who had already completed their training in nursing and excitedly told their stories, giving her the last push she needed to apply.

Grueling Training

In 1931, with the determination of a speeding train, she attempted to enter one of the region's oldest and proudest hospitals, St. Bartholomew's (also known simply as Barts) in central London. This training hospital ran in the voluntary sector (nonprofit), which contradicted heavily with its notoriously strict and limited student acceptance.

Turner recalls how the application interview was quite an ordeal because "each year nearly 50% of the girls who were interviewed for a nurse training place were rejected out of hand" (Starns, 2010), which didn't give any of them much confidence.

But rejection would not be Turner's fate because she was often described as fitting into the career with more ease than many others around her. Remember, she had already proclaimed her moral code as stoic and trustworthy. She had a strong stomach, worked long hours, and was always seen with a smile on her face. Everything about her demeanor suggested she was a caretaker.

Turner was accepted for the position of probationer nurse at the hospital that year, which meant she had a three-month trial period before being fully accepted into the program.

A probationer nurse's main responsibilities were to listen well, pass exams, and work hard—sometimes up to 72 hours a week. And when probationer nurses were not working, they were studying or sleeping. There was no time for anything else. Senior and matron nurses constantly monitored the probation nurses, scrutinizing their overall attitude and demeanor, as well as mental and physical health under stressful situations.

Turner lived in a communal home near the hospital with 500 other nurses. It was hard to say whether it was lingering impacts from the Great Depression or the strict hospital oversight, but restrictions were rampant throughout the commune. Bathe in lukewarm water (because hot water is bad for you). Do not toast your bread (because burnt toast is bad for you). These were some of the silly yet successful tricks to get the women to minimize water and electricity use and be as conservative as possible, thus saving the hospital money as well.

They would eat very starchy and cheap meals and not have much time for self-care. Most nurses put on weight in school, and many more would drop out in their first year either from sheer physical and mental exhaustion or homesickness.

The head matron, Miss Helen Day, who was responsible for accepting and declining potential nurses, was famously difficult to please and had a keen eye for cleanliness and discipline. "In 1931 nursing was an arduous profession with strict discipline and very little pay. The working day for Margot was 6:30 in the morning until 8:00 at night, with only one day off a month" (*QARANC*, 2021), which Turner seemed not to mind.

What was the daily routine of a probation nurse? She had to cover all the basic responsibilities that a nurse takes on throughout her career, such as:

- checking vitals every day

- serving patients food and drink

- washing patients down (bucket and cloth)

- changing bedding

- cleaning the *whole* ward

- emptying bedpans (what a joy)

- dressing wounds and applying kaolin poultices (anti-inflammatory and pain suppressant natural clay that is used mainly in animal healthcare today) to clear abscesses from infection

- applying whisked egg whites (the component of egg whites—amino acids—are helpful to increasing cell reformation on burns and other wounds) to sores to speed up the recovery rate.

- sterilizing equipment and instruments

- preparing operating theaters before surgeons arrived

- administering medication (oral and inter-vascular) with senior nursing supervision

These are just *some* of the duties they got through. It surely makes you think that whoever was able to endure the stress of training would certainly be able to endure war. The woman who walked the halls of Barts needed to be above vanity and pride.

It was not just the routine and daily practice of cleanliness, duty, discipline, and a rule-abiding attitude that needed to be present in a "Bart's nurse." She also needed to possess a natural air of emotional intelligence, modesty, professionalism, and overall obedience. After the probationary period, the nurses would begin their four years of training to become an RN (in America it was three years) and she took this in stride, passing all of her exams successfully and keeping her wits about her.

For nurses in training, life in the hospital was oppressive and monotonous, as expected, but their youth and excitement still remained. Over those four years, Turner built a strong friendship with her classmates, and they sometimes went to parties and danced at jazz bars. They received free tickets from the company to see theater shows or a new film. And since Turner loved sports, she would go swimming or ride horses whenever she could in order to clear her mind.

Letting down their hair was only natural, even though these women were instructed to always dress conservatively so as not to attract unnecessary male attention, because as we know, getting married or "falling pregnant" were circumstances that called for immediate dismissal from the program.

In 1935, at the age of 25, Turner finally wrote her last exam at Barts, qualifying as a State RN. Although she was now qualified, her pay barely increased, and she was still required to sign a contract to work at Barts for another six months.

She gained experience as an operating theater nurse (surgical nurse) and was asked to keep her position for another six months, due to her work ethic and soft touch. Just before Turner was due to sign a new contract, she made a choice that would change her life forever.

Turner's friend Nancy was visiting her sister, Eleanor, and Turner tagged along for the visit. Throughout the weekend, Eleanor would inspire Turner to pursue the QAs. Eleanor worked as a nurse in the services of Queen Alexandra's Imperial Military Nursing Corps and had just returned from a posting in a foreign country. She recalled all her adventures and experiences over those months.

Turner returned from that weekend away as a changed young woman. She was not going to sign the extension contract at Barts. No, she was going to sign up to join the QAs!

A few weeks later she declined the follow-up contract with grace and gratitude and made it straight to the Cambridge Military Hospital to begin her six-month probation training as an army nurse. Her training went off without a hitch, and a few months later, the 27-year-old was working comfortably at the Queen Alexandra Hospital Millbank in London as a general nurse. But she wanted to specialize further, and she wanted desperately to travel. She couldn't really say that her experience in the QAs had been that adventurous so far, as she hadn't even left England, but she waited patiently for an overseas posting to come her way.

In 1938, Turner got confirmation to depart aboard the troopship *Neuralia* on its three-week journey from England to Karachi, India (now Pakistan). The tensions in Europe were beginning to show, and the profitable yet unstable colony of India needed to be secured from civil unrest and the upcoming war. Therefore, the Empire sent military reinforcements and medics in anticipation and fear.

On the journey, the ship stopped at various locations, such as Gibraltar and Malta, to pick up more passengers and supplies, and refuel. The port dockings allowed Turner and the other nurses (along with civilians and servicemen) to briefly visit the cities before heading onwards.

Finally! she thought to herself.

She couldn't wait to head off into the unknown.

There...

"It's so noisy!" said a fellow nurse to Turner while they traveled from the chaotic port of Karachi to the hospital nearby. As they drove past markets filled with people, Turner could smell the intense aroma of spices, hear the energetic bargaining in their strange language, and was amazed by the vibrant colors of the robes the locals wore. The truck was constantly stopping on the dusty roads to allow cows to cross, and locals would stare at them while they waited.

"I quite like it. The smells and the sounds are mesmerizing. And look, the sun is shining!" Turner replied while still looking out the window.

"All right, Margot, we'll see if that's still your tune a couple of weeks from now," she said in irritation, while attempting to swat a fly away from her sweaty brow.

And in fact, Turner did relish every aspect of Eastern culture. The hum and buzz of Karachi were overwhelming to many women, but Turner found it peaceful and intensely spiritual.

New Lands, New Obstacles

Her first posting began at the Bareilly Military Hospital, which specifically catered to British military personnel. In India, communicable diseases weren't well controlled, meaning that the nurses had to travel to the patients to take care of them to prevent the disease's spread in the hospital unit. "Aside from the usual medical and surgical emergencies, the main medical conditions in India were smallpox, typhoid, cholera, and malaria" (Starns, 2010). Nurses, including Turner, were sometimes sent to these remote military camps (hill stations) to treat and stabilize patients from there and then had to travel all the way back to the main hospital.

By the following year in 1939, the ominous news of war was everywhere on the wireless, though Turner was too busy to take notice. Japan started to ruffle feathers in the Pacific, threatening and invading smaller regions one after another, moving ever closer from East to West.

Turner was then sent to work at the Ranikhet Hospital in northern India to treat the wounded there. Ranikhet was located just below the Himalayas, and the view was magnificent from the hospital's rooftop, which she faithfully went up to every morning to watch the sunrise over the enormous white peaks.

A few months later, Turner got the opportunity to work at the British Garrison Military Hospital in Meerut and specialize further in her favorite field of theater nursing, while implementing army operations. The arena of military surgical nursing was complex and strenuous, and naturally, one in which this gifted woman excelled.

*Figure 3: Dame Margot Turner Wearing Tropical Kit
Alongside an Indian Elephant*

*Photo permission from the Trustees of the Army Medical Services
Museum*

The theater nurse always needed to be alert and know
what the surgeon needed before he asked. Picture them
running around the operating room in scrubs, handing
over equipment and clean tools, wiping foreheads,

adjusting face masks and surgical caps, and administering IVs. A few nurses would specialize in sedation and become anesthetists.

Ironically, the fact that Turner was so good at what she did later became a detriment to her wanting to join the war efforts. The matron on her ward denied her application to enlist multiple times; nevertheless, her persistent request eventually gave way to her being posted at military hospitals on war duty.

In 1941, she arrived in Kuala Lumpur in Malay (now Malaysia) to join the N°17 Combined GH, where she was the nurse in charge of their operating theater. She worked in the ward for a couple of months before the Japanese troops started encroaching and bombs started flying. They had to evacuate south, and soon, which made for a Christmas Eve that Turner would never forget.

The N°17 unit quickly boarded a ship to an unknown location. The unit only found out where they were headed after having been on board for a few days, as the secrecy of the operation was paramount. Thus, after several days of chartering over the dangerous open ocean, they arrived in the port of Singapore. The unit was to be set up in a GH in Tanjong Malim until more news arrived.

These early days in Singapore were still relatively peaceful, even after the news of the Pearl Harbor bombing, as they didn't think that the Japanese would ever bomb the Malaya provinces. Sadly, this misunderstanding later cost thousands of lives. But in the interim, the nurses would head out to the Raffles

Hotel for parties and savor the British Empire's great city.

In the mid-20th century, Malay was known as British Malaya, which comprised the Federated Malay States, a very profitable territory of the British Empire. The British protectorates ruled the Malay Peninsula, as well as Singapore Island, and the Emperor of Japan was not going to let that last any longer.

After arriving at the British Military Hospital in Singapore, the unit was overwhelmed by the insurgency of injured British and Malayan soldiers who had been defending Singapore from the Japanese invasion. Turner mentioned in an interview that "you might get off for an hour or two in the evening then back to work again" (*QARANC*, 2021). Later, she was sent to Changi hospital to assist in evacuation duties of patients back to Singapore.

Due to the despicable accounts of Japanese troops raping and killing women, the Commanding officers chose to evacuate all the female staff again. There were nurses from Australia (Australian Army Nursing Corps) and British QAs in that hospital who were evacuated together with other women and children.

Many of the nurses did not want to leave their position in Singapore, seeing that so many people were dying, but they were ultimately forced to do a "lucky draw" from a hat to send nurses off on the *Empire Star* to the safer city of Batavia in the Dutch East Indies.

Turner and 50 other nurses were the last to be evacuated in February of 1942, but not before almost being killed in bomb raids that struck the Singapore Cricket Club where they were waiting for their ship, the *Kuala*, to arrive. Little did she know that she was about to embark not only on a literal ship of death, but on a figurative journey that would take her into the darkest and bleakest phase of her life.

Japanese Power

The *Kuala* is now overloaded with desperate people trying to get away from the massacre unfolding in Singapore. Turner manages to get aboard safely, but some nurses were not so fortunate and were bombed while attempting to embark.

All seems fine while they quietly navigate through the Sumatra waters to possible safety until they are spotted by a Japanese aircraft flying overhead. Panic hits when they hear the heavy rounds being shot at the vessel while huddling below deck. Then the captain makes the call to abandon ship, even though they know they don't have enough lifeboats or lifejackets to support all the passengers.

The officers proceed to pack as many nurses, women, and children as they can fit into the only two lifeboats available. Many more just jumped into the water and attempted to swim away from the flying bullets.

Fortunately, Turner is not stranded in the water. She is holding on to one of the overpacked lifeboats filled with crying babies and scared women. She watches as the flaming *Kuala* sinks into the depths of the Sumatran Straight. The Japanese aircraft proceeds to turn around and fire at all the people treading water, killing hundreds more.

Turner is one of the few nurses who manages to survive the ordeal, and she needs to assess the situation. She and the other survivors attach the two lifeboats and secure people in the water to the edge of the rafts as best as they can.

They take turns to sit and float and do their best to keep everyone alive. The survivors are finally able to disembark on an island called Pom Pong, where they attempt to survive for three days without clean water or food.

Many died from dehydration or their wounds. A bright light of hope arrived in the form of a British vessel that rescued the stranded survivors from the island. The nurses were asked to help the injured on that ship who had just been attacked. They were unsure of the next move; they knew the Japanese planes were on the lookout and that such an obvious vessel would be shot down in no time. But their clear duty was to help.

Not long after that, the English ship was shot down. Turner and 16 other survivors, including small children, were again stranded on rafts. Over the course of three more days, they floated aimlessly and every single person except Turner died. Children, mothers, the elderly, and the fatally wounded. "I examined each of them with great care before committing their little bodies to the sea. The last one was a very small baby and it was difficult to know when it was dead" (Sandilands, 1993).

Now utterly alone, Turner could only pray and conserve her energy as much as possible. She was so badly sunburned that when she was eventually rescued (or captured) by a Japanese ship, they could not recognize her as Caucasian. She was severely dehydrated but had managed to survive by cleverly collecting some rainwater in her makeup compact and eating some floating seaweed over those three days.

The Japanese doctor onboard spoke some English and was kind and considerate to her when he found out she was a nurse. He treated her with respect, and under his care she began a partial recovery. Did he know where she was destined to go next?

Initially, Turner was held in the Bangka Island camp with other women and children before being sent to the Sumatran mainland to join the main prison of Palembang.

The word *tenko* was the Japanese word for the headcount, a process these women had to endure daily standing under the scorching heat for hours, either with buckets on their heads or without any water.

Turner seemed to have a knack for getting into the Japanese soldiers' "bad books" and was beaten many times. During one beating, she lost a front tooth. She even spent six months in a specialized secret prison in the Pamberg camp that sequestered Allied spies (they were convinced she was one) and tortured the prisoners for information. Many prisoners were never returned to their cells. She recalls her experience there saying (*Dame Margot Turner*, n.d.):

The other prisoners were a rum lot, I don't know what they had done but they were good to me. They shared their food if they had any and they were considerate. There were so many unspeakable things going on. It is not something I really talk about much, the things they were doing to local people. You could hear the screams. There are some things that were unspeakable even in the books that are written about it. (para. 35)

The Japanese officials released Turner upon the realization that she was not, in fact, a spy and was therefore of no use to them. She was finally reunited with the other nurses in the main camp.

Starved, traumatized, and forced to bury a fellow camp internee every week, she was completely cut off from world news. She did not know that the Japanese cities of Nagasaki and Hiroshima had been devastated by atomic bombings in early August of 1945. Nor did she know why, all of a sudden, the Japanese soldiers were treating them with a little more humanity, feeding them actual food, abusing them less, and acting nervously.

Things would start making a little more sense over the next few weeks as most of the Japanese officers either fled their posts in the camp or committed suicide by *hara-kiri* (traditional Japanese sword suicide).

Not until mid-September of that year would the camp be spotted by Allied Air Force troops and the POWs rescued soon after. The Japanese had attempted to "fatten them up" before their rescue so as to eliminate the evidence of harsh starvation and mistreatment, hoping to lessen the punishment the Japanese Empire knew was soon to follow.

Turner and the other women were airlifted to the British Medical Hospital in Singapore where they would remain and recover for nine days before being sent back to Britain on the Polish ship *Sobieski*.

The month she spent onboard the ship heading back to her homeland was so vastly different from her past experiences. Now the journey was peaceful, without the fear of enemy discovery. Maybe it even felt a little empty, but at last, she was finally on her way home.

... And Back Again

After two months of leave spent with her mother in Hove, near Brighton, she needed to get back to duty. We might ask ourselves why she immersed herself in work again so soon after the prolonged trauma she had endured and all the tragedy she had witnessed at first hand.

We can only speculate; but what we do know is that she dealt with the consequences of war in her typical stoic manner, being strong for others, as she had always been. "Indeed, following the death of her father she had realized, perhaps more than most, the value of self-control and self-discipline. She considered displays of emotion to be a sign of weakness and self-indulgence" (Starns, 2010). With that perspective, perhaps we can theorize that stuffing emotions away was the most viable way for her to move forward in her life. And she did that with great purpose.

In 1946, along with the other female veterans of honor, Turner was awarded the Member of the Order of the British Empire (MBE). For the next 21 years, she would proceed to have a progressive and illuminating career within the QAs, continuing her overseas duties in Malta and Egypt as well as within Great Britain.

In 1957 she was invited to Buckingham Palace to be awarded the Royal Red Cross Medal by the Queen herself. She then progressed to the highest rank of Chief Military Nurse (Brigadier) in 1964, becoming a Dame (awarded the Most Excellent Order of the British Empire) the following year. And in 1968, she would retire as Colonel Commandant of the QAs, a title she would hold until 1974.

A book by Sir John Smyth titled *The Will to Live* gives the reader a detailed look at Turner's life. In the foreword, fellow WWII nurse Brigadier Barbara Gordon goes on to thank Turner for her service and mentions (1970):

> Margot was adamant that the book must be about the experiences and hardships suffered by all those Nursing Sisters and wives who were caught up in the horrors of those events which we call the Fall of Singapore. The joy and privilege of knowing Margot is for her modesty and her matter-of-fact acceptance that she did no more than hundreds of others did, or would have done in similar circumstances. (p. 10)

Turner appeared in the popular British TV series *This Is Your Life* in the late 1970s. She was very much against it when the family first mentioned to her that the producers wanted to interview her, but her family later "fooled" her into appearing.

The show brought together other nurses who were POWs with her in Sumatra and they told their individual stories, urging Turner to do the same. They all sang wartime songs together and embraced, emotional about the memories and stories brought back to life (*Brigadier Margot Turner*, n.d.):

> In the event, as the program unfolded, they were admirable. They told their stories with brevity and humor then withdrew gracefully to take their places with the rest of the guests. There was no suggestion of the extraordinary revelation that was in the offering as the program came to its end. (para. 8)

Margot Turner passed away in 1993 in a home for disabled veterans at St. Dunstan's in Brighton. She was 83 and left behind no family. What she did leave were strong friendships, and more importantly, a strong legacy that stands true today. A sharp reminder of the power of women's resourcefulness, she coped with the most extreme situations with pragmatism and strength.

She was meant to command the room, which she did without the pervasive higher ranking attitude one commonly saw in Brigadiers or Colonels. She was a natural-born leader whose place in WWII meant so much more for other people than for herself.

During this time, women mastered the skills of quiet confidence and clever decision-making to fight sexism in their ranks. While Margot Turner may not have fully grasped the impact of all she and her nurse colleagues contributed at the time, we can all (men and women) appreciate the gains today. And we can recognize that women, especially women of color, are still fighting this battle.

Chapter 4:

Vivian Bullwinkel

By now her unit could pack and unpack the hospital quickly and efficiently with their eyes closed. And sometimes they had to do it in complete darkness, so yes, it was almost like having your eyes closed.

She arrived in this foreign land with a willingness to serve, learn, and save as many people as her two hands could manage. But before she knew it, the honorable deed turned into one of absolute mayhem and desperation.

When did they lose so much control over their borders? she wonders. These Japanese troops were relentless and fierce, doing far more damage than necessary and continually pushing the Allied armies and hospitals further south.

Their medical unit couldn't possibly save everyone. That was the biggest tragedy of it all! There were just too few hands, too few resources, and too few ways to escape. It was a constant struggle and balancing act between saving your own skin over that of your patient. Soldiers came first, but it was complicated because if there were no medics to treat them, then how could the troops keep up their strength and numbers?

At first, the bombs were terrifying, dropping so close that her teeth would rattle in her skull, her heart would stop, and her body freeze. After she had been in the situation for a while, she found it altogether numbing. She'd hear the bomb, thank the heavens she was still alive, and keep on moving and prioritizing her duties.

A year ago she never would have imagined that the screams of horror and pain would become such familiar sounds. Yet she would be surprised even more by her newfound strength. Her movements were so automated and practiced that she knew her part of the flow in the wards even apart from tending to her patients—her communication with her nursing sisters and her reliance on the army to alert them of danger.

She realized that this… this was what real team effort looked like.

The Venture

Vivian Statham Bullwinkel was born in 1915 in Kapunda, South Australia. Her father, George Albert Bullwinkel, was originally from Essex, England. He had immigrated to Australia to work on a cattle ranch as a jackeroo (farmhand). Her mother, Eva Shagog, was Australian by birth.

Bullwinkel's grandparents on her mother's side lived in Adelaide, where the 9-year-old and her younger brother John would eventually move. Her grandfather was a police officer within the South Australian Police Force, which heavily instilled in her the regard for duty and rank.

Her friends and family would affectionately call her "Bully" for her strong, athletic physique and height, not to mention her gregarious attitude.

In later years, she returned to her parent's town of Broken Hill, all the way out in the infamous outback, where she had attended a local high school and later, in 1934, had joined the Broken Hill District Hospital to train as a midwife and nurse.

After graduating, she moved to Hamilton, Victoria, to work at the Kia-Ora Hospital. In 1939, she would receive extensive training in casualty nursing before the infamous announcement boomed over the radio waves in September of that year. Australian Prime Minister, Robert Menzies, solemnly declared (*Australians in WWII*, n.d.):

> Fellow Australians, it is my melancholy duty to inform you officially, that in consequence of a persistence by Germany in her invasion of Poland, Great Britain has declared war upon her and that, as a result, Australia is also at war. No harder task can fall to the lot of a democratic leader than to make such an announcement. (para. 2)

A Time To Try

Australia had just gained independence from the British Empire, and citizens worried about their future political stability and relative security as a new nation. Australia's forces would never have been able to defend their Pacific theater against Japan without assistance from

Great Britain. The irony was not lost on the Brits nor the Aussies. For a brief moment, Australia was relying on its former colonizer for protection, and Britain was exercising authority that it had technically relinquished to control the Australian front.

Either way, the war was upon them, and the Australian government, like many others, worried about the sheer lack of medical staff available to cope with the insurgence of healthcare needs the imminent war would bring.

Bullwinkel saw directly through to the heart of nursing and she decided to enlist as soon as she could. She was sent over to the Jessie McPherson Hospital in Melbourne where she worked in the operating theater for a while before proactively attempting to join the Armed Forces.

The 26-year-old Bullwinkel applied to enter the Royal Australian Air Force (RAAF) but was rejected because of the shape of her feet.

Flat feet are a natural formation of the body where the arch of the foot is less pronounced. In the 20th century, recruiters considered flat feet to be more than just an inconvenience, and anyone (man or woman) who "suffered" from this malformation of the foot was immediately rejected from military service. The prevailing opinion of the time was that this condition was a sign of low breeding and poor health. This misconception would thankfully change years later.

Although Bullwinkel was left in the dust for a while, she was still motivated to keep looking for a way in. Surely if they were so desperate to staff the war, they would overlook such a silly "defect"!

Sure enough, she was accepted under the Australian Army Nursing Service (AANS) later that year and was immediately posted to the island of Singapore with her new unit.

There...

Vivian Bullwinkel joined the main 2/13th Australian GH unit in Singapore that September, and over four months, she got a taste of what life was like under the Japanese occupation. She also worked at other wards within the 2/10th AGH for some time before returning to her initial unit in Johor Bahru.

Figure 4: Studio Portrait of Staff Nurse Vivian Bullwinkel,
AANS, 1941

AUSTRALIAN WAR MEMORIAL   P03960.001

That December of 1941, as we discovered in Margot
Turner's story, the Japanese advanced further south and
invaded Malaya, forcing residents of all northern towns
to evacuate to the closest and safest city in the south,

Singapore. Here we can see the stories of Vivian Bullwinkel and Margot Turner converge, which gives us a glimpse into the friendship and camaraderie the British and Australian nurses would build with one another in the desperate years to follow.

The 2/13th scrambled for safer locations to set up their wards and found space at the St. Patrick's school. These premises needed to become a hospital in a matter of days, with the staff working tirelessly for weeks to set up. A few weeks later, the Japanese entered Singapore, forcing the makeshift hospital to evacuate once again, as "plans changed quickly and the defense of the island ended in defeat ordering Bullwinkel and 65 fellow nurses to escape" (Jakubenko, 2021).

As we know, thousands of civilians and military personnel would die during that deadly week, but Bullwinkel would be one of the lucky few to escape with her life on an unlucky Friday the 13th of February 1942.

The Island

The staff hastily boarded an overloaded steamer ship, the *SS Vyner Brooke*, which was heading for a quick escape to Sumatra through the Strait of Banks. Along with the nurses on board, there were more than 200 civilians and a good number of English military personnel and staff.

It took two days for the ship to be spotted, followed, and strafed (bombed) by cruising Japanese aircraft passing between Borneo and Sumatra. Even as the ship was under severe siege, Bullwinkel still managed to write down her thoughts and experiences in real time! A recount from her diary entry states matter-of-factly (Jakubenko, 2021):

> Beautiful sunny morning. Calm sea and anchored. Very pretty island. Peacefulness disturbed as planes flew over and machine-gunned boat. All took to lower deck as pre-arranged, but raid all over and much discussion on planes sinking us and enemy aircraft. Took up anchor and steamed along. 2 pm air raid siren. All down to lower deck and flattened down. Six planes attack once more, bombs hit, second, third time. Third bomb below the waterline. Whistle for all on deck to take lifeboats. Wight, Nourse, Cuthberston, several civilians injured… (para. 7)

In absolute panic, people pushed and rushed to save their own lives. Many were gunned down on the ship, some in the water, and others drowned, including 12 AANS nurses. The lifeboats bobbed in open water for days with women, children, and some personnel guided by the current towards the Eastern Sumatran island of Bangka, namely Radji Beach.

Over 100 people were stranded on the beach, with 53 nurses, 60 servicemen, and some civilian women and children all awaiting their fates. Tragically, they would soon discover that the island offered no safe refuge from the dangerous waters.

Floating debris and dead bodies swept up on the shore along with some survivors, the 20 or so English soldiers from another ship that escaped their own attack by the Japanese aircraft.

This was not a time to feel sorry for themselves, but rather to step up and do whatever they could for these people. The group knew that the Japanese would eventually find them, one way or another, so they decided to surrender rather than hide; they didn't want to wait for the inevitability of being found. In fact, one of the officers from the steamship volunteered to go look for the Japanese camp and offer their peaceful surrender with the intention of being captured.

The castaways were relying on a WWII "code of conduct" that stipulated how non-combatants, such as nurses, civilians, and injured soldiers, were to be protected and treated fairly and humanely by the enemy forces if captured. This agreement was (mostly) held up by the Allied forces and some Axis units, but the Japanese hadn't exactly embraced the concept that Western POWs were to be treated with respect. Bullwinkel and the rest would soon find out that this particular Japanese troop was not going to honor the group's protected status.

While the scouting soldier was away looking for the enemy camp, Bullwinkel and the remaining nurses, headed by army matron Irene Drummond, who also trained at Broken Hill, proposed that the civilian women, some nurses, and children head straight for the nearby village of Muntok and calmly surrender so they could receive water and food while they took care of the injured soldiers on the beach.

The nurses proceeded to set up a temporary triage area that evening for other survivors that washed up on shore, building up a makeshift tent. They made sure to emphasize their neutrality by displaying a large red cross on the tent, and purposely wearing their Red Cross armbands at all times as extra precaution.

When the investigative soldier returned the next day with 20 Japanese soldiers, a horrifying act of brutality occurred that would come to be known as the Bangka Island Massacre.

"*Issho ni josei!*" then roughly, "Women together!" shouted one of the Japanese soldiers to the group of nurses in the triage tent.

Bullwinkel and the others walked out slowly holding their hands up in submission, acutely aware of the rifles and large cruel-looking knives pointed at them. The vocal officer was clearly the man in charge as he then shouted orders to his men in Japanese. They proceeded to manhandle the 22 nurses and one civilian woman together and push them down to sit on the sand. Bullwinkel apprehensively looked at the others and dared not say a word.

The enemy troops then rounded up all the officers (around 60 men) and roughly split them into two groups. They took one group of frail and desperate men and motioned for them to walk around the cove of the beach out of sight of the nurses. Minutes passed and the Japanese men eventually returned alone casually wiping down their bayonets. Then they proceeded to take the second group of men, who by now knew their fate. But as soon as the injured Allied soldiers hobbled past the cove and saw the dead bodies floating in the water, horror set in.

The group of women cowering on the beach first heard the commotion and then the sound of rifles firing. The Japanese shot them all dead and then killed off the remaining survivors with their bayonets.

Australian and British soldiers and crewmen were killed in cold blood on the beach that day. These men were meant to become POWs, as per the wartime regulation under the Second Geneva Convention. But no concern or care was given to the "rules of war."

Wartime conduct violations happened frequently throughout WWII. The Axis forces may have committed more offenses, but the criminal acts committed by Allied forces should not be overlooked. Some countries abided by the humane reason for creating the rule, while others found easy loopholes to cause as much suffering and death as they deemed fit.

Back on the beach, in a sadistic move of dominance and fearmongering, the Japanese soldiers sat by the nurses, calmly wiping down their knives and cleaning the blood splatters off their rifles while speaking to each other about what to do next.

Outside of the nurses' view, a machine gun was being set up.

The nurses and the civilian woman who were huddled together were unsure what would happen next. Until now they had assumed that they would be spared, but now, looking at the blood on the sand, they were not so sure.

The Japanese commander then instructed the 22 nurses and civilian women to stand up and make a line on the beach. The water sloshed into their shoes. They were commanded to walk into the surf up to their waistlines with their backs to the beach and look into the horizon. We cannot possibly know what went through their minds but it is easy to imagine that panic set in.

A few seconds later, that machine gun further up on the beach roared to life, spewing bullets into their backs. Up and down it swept and gunned down all the women, leaving them to bleed out in the water... an easy way to wash away evidence.

By sheer luck or fortunate positioning, Bullwinkel was the only woman to survive this barbaric execution. "I was towards the end of the line and the bullet that hit me struck me at the waist and just went straight through" (Zinn, 2000). She described taking the bullet like being kicked by a large mule. Although the wound caused her to lose some blood, none of her vital organs were hit.

She pretended to be dead in the sand for a good 10 minutes, while her comrades lay motionless beside her or floated lifelessly out to sea. The waves mercilessly swept over her, and she tried her best to stay as still as possible.

The Japanese soldiers departed and left Bullwinkel alone on the beach. She slowly regained some strength and rose to her feet, bewildered and looking around her in anguish.

Unfortunately, there was no time to mourn, so she hobbled off into the jungle looking for cover and freshwater, making slow progress due to her loin injury. She discovered a British soldier hiding in the thick brush. He had narrowly escaped the Japanese massacre earlier that day and was suffering from a severe abdominal injury from a brutal gunshot. This was Private George Kingsley, a crew member on the *SS Vyner Brooke*.

The need to care for someone else was what kept Bullwinkel alive, despite her own injury. The two of them huddled together for 12 long days with Bullwinkel scrounging around for food, begging locals for scraps of food whenever she could, and sneaking off to retrieve water.

Injured and traumatized, the pair remained hidden and waited for as long as they could.

"George, we have to get you to proper medical care," Bullwinkel said to Private Kingsley that evening in the Sumatran jungle. "That wound is getting worse, and I need to address my own injury. We have to surrender."

"They will kill us, Vivian," he replied weakly.

"Can we live out here much longer before being discovered? This territory could be in their hands for years, George. Let's be rational," she replied. She had to take matters into her own hands.

The two hobbled into the town of Muntok out of sheer hunger and desperation. Bullwinkel was separated from Private Kingsley. She never saw him again. He soon died from his injuries, as he did not receive any medical care and barely any food.

Bullwinkel and the other civilian women were left to rot in barracks in Muntok for months. The women constantly fought off Japanese men who requested they join the brothels in town (as a more "comfortable" way to live) while living on one bowl of rice and some cold tea each day.

She painstakingly hid the fact that she was injured, by holding a water bottle over the hole in her dress where the bullet had entered. She feared that if the Japanese knew she was a surviving witness to a massacre, they would shoot her on the spot. She managed to recover some of her strength under the watchful eyes of the other nurses present. During those three years, they kept each other sane through their caretaking work.

The Prison

Bullwinkel and the others were then shipped off to mainland Sumatra and ordered to march for 12 hours upriver to the town of Palembang. Many more died on that trek due to the brutality of the soldiers, who killed anyone who fell behind (usually the weak and wounded).

From there, the men were sent to the actual jail at Palembang and the women lived under bamboo and palm leaf huts (open prisons) that protected little from the wet and cold environment. To make matters worse, these civilized women had to use trench toilets and sleep on the muddy floor.

Bullwinkel and her sisters suffered at the hands of the Japanese for two main reasons. First, their Red Cross parcels of medical and food supplies did not reach them, whether due to the Japanese military not detailing the location of the prison camps, or the prison guards stealing the contents for themselves. As a result, the prisoners became severely emaciated, and many died from malnutrition.

Second, the prison camp conditions were harsh, and the guards treated the prisoners very poorly. No clean water meant that people contracted tropical diseases, and the laborious work they were ordered to do was far greater than the caloric energy they received from food. Male POWs were expected to build houses, airfields, railways, and the like for the Japanese Armed Forces, and the women to conform to slightly lighter labor.

Bullwinkel and 31 other British and Australian nurses (Turner included), stayed for three and a half long years with the other civilian men, women, and children. Their nurse training was what enabled them to survive and keep the others from deteriorating past the point of no return. She recalls, "We were self-reliant people. We certainly had not had any training before we went to war, but we went along and learned how to stay alive" (Zinn, 2000).

Bullwinkel was fiercely protected by the other women in the prison camp. They had heard of her story on Bangka Island and knew that they couldn't let her die.

As the sole survivor, she needed to live to tell the world about the Bangka Island massacre and the atrocities that occurred in the camps.

The days were long and desperately difficult, but Bullwinkel tried not to let herself plummet into hopelessness. A postcard, the only one she ever sent, arrived at her mother's postbox in Australia just before the war ended, detailing their struggles, but never undermining their strength. She most notably writes, "My roving spirit has been somewhat checked" (Jakubenko, 2021). She had seen enough of the world for a while and dreamed of home.

The women laughed, joked, formed illicit choirs, and kept their spirits high in any way they could. Keeping to the routine and the structure the nurses enforced helped them all to stay busy and kept their minds occupied. A descent into mental breakdown had to be held at bay at all costs.

When the Japanese surrendered in September of 1945, also known as V-J Day (Victory over Japan Day), Bullwinkel weighed 70 lbs. For a woman of 5 feet 6 inches tall, it bordered on skeletal.

Figure 5: Rescued POWs From the 2/10th and 2/13th ANS Units, 1945

She and her Australian compatriots were not immediately returned home because they were far too thin, as author Ian Shaw describes: "The army representatives said if we [they] send these nurses back to Australia with an average of 30 kilos, the people will demand that we start mass executions of Japanese prisoners" (Bissland, 2022).

So off they went back to Singapore, namely the St. Patrick's Hospital, where they had worked earlier in the war. They remained there until they were in better health and then shipped back home.

"By the time the war was over, a total of more than 30,000 POWs died from starvation, disease, and mistreatment—both within and outside of the Japanese Mainland" (*Information about the Prisoners of War*, n.d.).

... And Back Again

Vivian Bullwinkel returned to cheers and congratulations when she disembarked in Melbourne in December of 1945 along with the other 23 nurses. Her memories, fresh with trauma, were to be detailed to a court of law very soon.

Figure 6: Informal Group Portrait of AANS Homecoming, Sister Bullwinkel Second From the Left

In 1946, the Allied forces created the International Military Tribunal (IMT) to address the Nazi war crimes and the International Military Tribunal Far East (IMTFE) to address those of the Japanese.

The IMTFE, also called the Tokyo War Crimes Tribunal, was held in the Japanese capital where Bullwinkel and other camp survivors gave testimony on the occurrences on the Sumatran beach. Consequently, "the Japanese sergeant was charged and served 12 years imprisonment for his part in the killings, and the captain in charge of the murderous troop committed suicide while he was being held for questioning" (Bissland, 2022).

Figure 7: Captain Vivian Bullwinkel Sitting Witness at the War Crimes Tribunal, 1946

AUSTRALIAN WAR MEMORIAL   P04585.003

The testimony Bullwinkel gave, however, was not the whole story. Years later, she revealed publicly that the women were not only mistreated and underfed during those three years of imprisonment, but they were also raped multiple times by the Japanese officers. Painfully embarrassed and humiliated, she later also admitted that she and the 23 women on Radji Beach were violated before they were massacred. She kept the secret to honor their memory.

The Australian government was well aware of this information, but due to the societal taboo around rape at the time and a sense of collective guilt about the crimes, she and many others were ordered to keep that information to themselves when speaking in Tokyo.

A total of 78 AANS nurses were killed through field duty or some kind of tropical illness, with the most prevalent cause being mistreatment in POW camps.

A year later, Bullwinkel retired from the military as Lieutenant Colonel and joined the Fairfield Infectious Disease Hospital in Melbourne where she worked for over 30 years. During this time, she joined many committees to raise funds for the nurses' families who died in the Bangka Massacre. She also became a council member at the Australian War Memorial in Canberra (the first female) and then president of the Australian College of Nursing.

In 1955, 40-year-old Bullwinkel joined the Citizen Military Forces working as a veteran nurse and in 1975, she assisted in the Vietnamese war treating the thousands of local orphans airlifted to Australia.

At 62 years of age, Bullwinkel was now Director of Nursing at Fairfield Hospital in Melbourne and was about to be a married woman too. She tied the knot with Colonel Francis West Statham and they moved to Perth to live out the rest of their days.

In the years that ensued, Bullwinkel (now Statham) received honors (albeit late) for her service in WWII. She was appointed Member of the Order of The British Empire (MBE) in 1973 and also an Officer of the Order of Australia (OA) in 1993. She received stars, medals, honors, and declarations that she did not always believe she deserved, most importantly, the Florence Nightingale Medal of service.

In 2000, at the age of 84, she died of a heart attack. Four veteran nurses attended her state funeral.

Vivian Bullwinkel Statham's legacy was remarkable; it demonstrates something even greater than service— respect for those who never made it out. She kept silent and was tortured by her terrible secrets and memories from the war, but she kept her head high, continuing to work and honor her profession. She was not only strong, but resilient and determined.

Associations and institutions have dedicated their buildings and campuses to her, namely the Vivian Bullwinkel Wing of Perth Hollywood Private Hospital and The Vivian Bullwinkel Lodge, a care facility in north Perth. There is also a foundation in her name at the Australian College of Nursing called the Bullwinkel Project.

After Bullwinkel's death, her story became the subject of a documentary made by Australian national TV, as well as several books and articles. Hollywood made references to her and the other nurses in the 1997 film *Paradise Road,* starring Australian actor Cate Blanchett and American actor Glenn Close as victims of WWII POWs in the Sumatran camps.

The film depicts the choirs the women prisoners formed. They wrote entire musical scores from memory and even gave concerts for the camp guards and commanders. All gatherings were forbidden, but the guards usually let the concerts happen and even came to listen. Dame Margot Turner also recalled these moving concerts in interviews.

As the nurses' history is timeless, we can only hope that their stories are soon represented again in a modern film to remind people of the horrors and triumphs that took place during WWII.

"Meanwhile at Radji Beach, where the massacre occurred, now stands a plaque marking one of the Second World War's atrocities, which might have passed unrecorded but for the determination of its sole survivor" (Zinn, 2000), who placed it there when she visited seven years before her death.

Today, the beach is called English Bay by the locals, as a reminder of the atrocities that transpired there. It is said that locals discovered bones washing ashore many years later, and fishermen would not cast their nets or line anywhere nearby, in superstitious and respectful fear.

If the gunner on that beach had fired longer at the end of the line, or if Bullwinkel had been standing mere inches to the left or right, she would likely have perished right then and there alongside the others in the lineup. No one would ever know that massacre took place except the perpetrators, who are now likely dead.

One can only wonder how many incidents occurred during the Second World War that left no survivors to bear witness to the brutality committed, nor honor for those who were lost and forgotten.

Thanks to these incredible women—their will to live, their strength, their resilience, their courage—we know the truth of war.

The Canadian Royal Army Medical Corps

Canada was forever transformed after WWII, and for better reasons than you might think. When the war ended, the country exponentially increased its commitment to world affairs and became a prosperous nation through industrialization and urbanization. The trauma of war was the fire that allowed Canada to bloom anew.

The Nursing Sisters of Canada were called Bluebirds for the distinctive color of the uniform they wore in WWI. The sky-blue shirt, the white apron and veil, and the brown belt gave them a soft and gentle appearance. But because that uniform was actually cumbersome and stiff, they altered it early in WWII to a more comfortable and practical look—pants and no veil.

Formation of the RCAMC

Things had changed drastically from their participation in the campaigns of WWI to those of WWII. For one, Canadians were no longer under British rule. They could and did send out self-sufficient armed and medical forces responsible for the Canadian troops posted overseas.

The Royal Canadian Army Medical Corps (RCAMC) was initiated in 1919 after many years of changing the various components of its organization. These changes allowed Canada to stand on its own two feet and really understand what its government and people were capable of.

In 1939, a policy was approved whereby "the care and treatment of sick and wounded personnel of the Canadian Active Service Force (CASF) would be undertaken by the Royal Canadian Army Medical Corps (RCAMC) rather than facilities provided by the British government" (Abra, 2012). After quickly realizing that their healthcare system was severely understaffed for the oncoming war, the Canadian government pushed for doctors and nurses to enlist in the military.

Recruiting and Mobilizing Efforts

Canadian nurses responded in droves. There was such a long volunteering list to enter military units that the government had to hold the waiting list for quite a long time, rejecting civilian nurses more often than not. Rejection did not deter these amazing Canadian women, who simply decided to enlist with either the British, South African, or American nursing services instead.

By 1942 the RCAMC had grown into two of Canada's military branches—the Royal Canadian Air Force Medical Services (RCAMS) and the Royal Canadian Naval Medical Services (RCNMS)—and members were stationed from France to Italy, and Belgium to Hong Kong.

Thanks to their extensive involvement in nursing years prior to WWII, the Canadian nurses found themselves already well-equipped and experienced in the military field of nursing and jumped straight on board the ships to overseas camps. "Between Canada and overseas, the Nursing Sisters worked in over 100 major hospital units" (*Canada's WW2 Nursing Sisters*, 2015), which are named simply by their number (N°). And because the Canadian Chain of Evacuation was very efficient, they were often dispatched to more specific "hot zones" in the war to speed up the triage and evacuation process.

The Best of the Best

The Field Hospital (FH) units located a couple of miles from the battlefield that received the first wounded quickly trickled down the patients to the Evacuation Hospitals (EH) a little further away in the encampment. Patients were then sent by ambulance, plane, train, or ship to the Station Hospitals (SH) for possible surgery, or off to recovery at the General Hospitals (GH) in main cities nearby or (if lucky) back home.

Within the EH units were niche units on hospital ships with specific fleets focused on retrieving bombed Allied troops and treating them onboard, as well as train hospitals that would pick up evacuees in the hundreds. And just like the Australians, Canadians had "flying ambulances" or air hospital units that bravely battled the skies to save men's lives.

The operation was like nothing seen on earth, and the Canadian Armed forces were well-positioned to cope. They had doctors and sisters with nerves of steel who worked tirelessly in the foreign countries under fierce fire, often ill-equipped yet still proficient.

Inez Williams, a Canadian WWII nurse, recalls her time

in France and the stark differences between a GH and FH (*Women in the military*, 2021):

> In the field, the entire unit was placed under canvas. The wards were made in the shape of an E, each ward with an average of 75 beds. Patients were classified according to the severity of their wounds to compile a priority list for surgery. Dressings were done in order on admission by the doctor in charge. After surgery, and after the removal of the first dressing, the nurse usually did the necessary treatments. (para. 18)

From their efforts all along the East and West coasts of Canada and well into their campaigns across the globe, they fought by land, air, and sea to protect what they understood as freedom. The Canadian forces were a major contributor to the Allied power, by injecting over 1.1 million men and women into the war. They outperformed their roles in the European theater, experiencing novelties and near-death experiences throughout the war.

Looking at the most basic statistics we find that by the end of the war "4,480 Canadian Nursing Sisters served in the military, 3,656 in the Army, 481 with the Air Force, and 343 with the Navy" (*Canada's WW2 Nursing Sisters*, 2015). Like all the Allied countries, their nurses went above and beyond, as we'll soon see in the stories of Jessie Middleton and Elizabeth Lowe—two Canadian women on a similar journey but with quite different experiences in the units in which they were posted.

Chapter 5:

Jessie Middleton
& Elizabeth Lowe

Jessie was often amazed at the difference between being on duty and being off duty, what it meant to work and what it meant to play. The contrast blew her mind every time she spent a few minutes thinking about it.

She had been in this idyllic town in central Italy for weeks now. They had managed to lodge their field hospital nice and snug within an old monastery off the beaten path while they waited for ambulances to ferry the remaining patients.

Most days were busy and rushed, while some days were so quiet and uneventful that she almost thought the war was over. She certainly didn't complain when she walked out of her sleeping tent with the other nurses and gazed upon the beautiful Mediterranean countryside.

Sure, she didn't have running water or warm cooked food. And sure, she washed her hair, her body, and her clothes in the same old tin army hat that was issued to her years prior. It was true she barely slept and was looking the worse for wear every time she peered at herself in her small compact mirror. But that did not dissuade her from enjoying this marvelous country and all the people she met and helped.

She saw death daily and heard cries of pain most nights, but she also saw love, kindness, and compassion in everyday experiences too. The girls in the unit were real friends, and the doctors were calm and thorough.

So what did she have to complain about? Some women were posted in Japan, some in Russia, and some in North Africa. She was lucky enough to find herself in a heavenly spot in hellish times.

Their Venture

Jessie Annie Lee Middleton was born in 1916 in a small community in the region of Langley in British Columbia (BC), Canada, then called Langley Prairie. Today it's known as Murrayville.

She was the last of eleven siblings born to father James Lee, a farmer, and mother Edith Brown. She attended the local high school in Langley and always knew that nursing was going to be in her future.

Her two eldest brothers fought in WWI against the Germans within the French territories. When she was just 8 years old, tragedy struck her family, taking one of her nephews as a baby. His death greatly affected her attitude toward health and caretaking.

In the opposite direction, way out on the east coast of Canada, we find Elizabeth Burnham Lowe. She was born the same year as Middleton, but in a small village called Renforth in New Brunswick, Canada, situated on the south banks of the Kennebecasis River.

Lowe would respond to the very same push to enlist in the war efforts as Middleton and she was geared up to serve her country as soon as the winds of war began to blow again in 1939.

Canadian Nursing Sister Hallie Sloan, who also joined the RCAMC in WWII, enlightened her interviewer by saying (Timeline, 2018):

> I think everyone was caught up in the fever of war, and well I guess, there was excitement, because people were joining up! And well my own brother had been in the Navy for some time and my father had been with the engineers for a long time.

As Sloan alluded to, both Middleton and Lowe felt the pressure of doing their bit for the war efforts. It clearly influenced the inspired nurses who were looking for adventure and experience but would soon find out what that really meant.

A True Calling

Middleton and Lowe went on to study nursing and await their chance to see the world. Middleton's early career was much better documented in the historical records, so we'll start there.

Jessie Middleton enrolled in the Royal Columbian Hospital in New Westminster as a junior nurse. She began her training in 1936 and spent three years in the program before graduating in September 1939, literally the day after Canada declared war on Germany.

Figure 8: Young Jessie Middleton in Her Bluebird Uniform

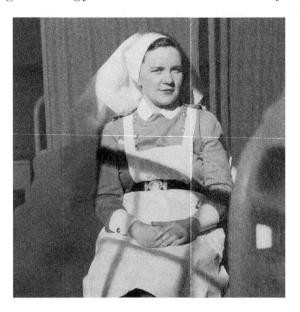

We theorize that Lowe graduated around the same time as Middleton, and from there, we know she worked at Winnipeg Hospital before being recruited into the RCAMC in 1940.

The allure of the RCAMC was not only the adventure of overseas duty, but also relatively good pay. A paycheck of $150 with boarding and food included was particularly appealing to any ambitious young woman.

They both would have been around 23 by the time they graduated, and while Lowe immediately jumped into overseas service, Middleton recalls having to wait till she turned 25. This is somewhat confusing, as the age criteria stood between 21 and 36, and she could have happily enlisted earlier.

Either way, while Middleton waited for her time to enlist, she was stationed at the Vancouver General Hospital in the maternity ward delivering babies. Some of the women she helped were of Japanese descent, and ever since the Japanese Empire had declared war on the West, they were seen as enemies and treated as such.

Even before WWII, racism was rife between Canadian nationals and Japanese people who had emigrated to Canada. Then when Japan bombed Pearl Harbor, social stigmas and fears got out of hand.

"Beginning in early 1942, the Canadian government detained and dispossessed more than 90% of Japanese Canadians, some 21,000 people, living in British Columbia" (Marsh, 2012). This distrust and fear spread like wildfire across Canada, whose government took some drastic steps to implement Japanese internment (detention or incarceration) while the war played out. The story of Japanese internment in the US was much the same.

Many of those detained were Canadian citizens by birth, but because they looked like the enemy, they were automatically treated as such—imprisoned behind high fences with no running water or fresh food, and if they did not comply, then they would get shipped off to POW camps in Ontario or Lake Superior. Only in 1988 did the Canadian government acknowledge the mistreatment and formally apologize for its actions towards its Japanese citizens and their families.

When Middleton finally entered the service in 1942, she was commissioned as Lieutenant Nursing Sister Lee under the Royal Canadian Army Medical Corps (RCAMC).

She worked on Vancouver Island at the Nanaimo GH, assisting the troops to recover from basic training injuries and overall illness, which was a good start, but gave no hint of what Middleton would later face.

She spent roughly six months working at the military hospital (MH) of Prince Rupert in B.C. in 1943. They lived in fear that the Japanese would attack their port, which was heavily monitored by large searchlights and also protected by an anti-submarine net. This posting would be her first authentic experience of wartime nursing.

Middleton visited her mother a few weeks before her departure for Scotland in March of that year, but she didn't tell her mother about the posting so she wouldn't fret. Her mother, however, quickly suspected that her daughter would be leaving the Canadian shores for the first time and was anxious she might never see her again. Mothers always seem to know.

Middleton soon received official news of her posting to the N°7 Canadian General Hospital (CGH) and boarded a train for Halifax, on the East coast of Nova Scotia to prepare to depart for Scotland.

Lowe, who had been working at the N°5 Canadian General Hospital (CGH) in Winnipeg, received her call to return to Nova Scotia in 1940.

One of the Nursing Sisters in the N°5 CGH unit joyfully expressed (Abra, 2012):

> Imagine with me, the excitement of the first nursing sisters to leave home for the war zone then you will realize how we felt in June, 1940. Our first thrill was a troop train, just like the pictures we had seen in newsreels or books and we were actually part of this vast movement. (p.43)

Lowe sailed on the *Duchess of Bedford* to Liverpool in 1940, which is where she heard about the Nazi invasion of France. It understandably filled her with dread while they peacefully and comfortably cruised to war.

In 1943, Middleton embarked on the *Queen Elizabeth* liner headed for the town of Greenock in Scotland. The liner was packed with servicemen, nurses, and civilians. Space constraints below deck left men sleeping out on the deck in the damp, cold, and unforgiving winds of the North Atlantic. Some of them contracted pneumonia during the journey.

Both Lowe and Middleton would experience anxiety as they sailed toward Europe at quite distinct stages of the war. The first arrived in controlled readiness as the war was just starting, while the latter arrived in more chaotic conditions amidst the constant fear of attack by German U-boats and fighter planes.

There...

"When in the heavens are they ever going to send us out? Really! I mean, we have been here for three years," Lowe said to her fellow nurse while she fussed over gauze in the casualty ward.

"You'll see, Elizabeth. Soon enough the call will come. Matron Pence said it'd be any day now," the other nurse replied in a typically calm Canadian fashion.

"Eh? She has been saying 'any day now' for the last two years!" Lowe said sarcastically, exaggerating the Canadian accent to tease the older matron. They both giggled and kept on working.

Unit N°5 CGH traveled from Liverpool into Taplow, to the west of London, to reside in the beautiful Ascot manner and work in the CGH within that area. Here they worked some incredibly long hours with some units receiving up to 600 injured men in a 19-hour timeframe. Many staff members barely had enough time to eat and drink before jumping right back into duty.

Meanwhile, Middleton recalls arriving in Scotland in 1943 saying, "Some of them [servicemen] never set foot on English soil - they were carried ashore on stretchers and sent straight back to Canada" to be treated for severe pneumonia (Florence, 2015).

From there, Middleton boarded another train headed for London, where her unit, the N°7 CGH, would also be based off the river Thames in the town of Taplow where they would receive more intense military training. As one nurse recalls (Timeline, 2018):

> Here we were, women, we were strong, carrying 40lbs of gear and as we were going towards the train in marching order. And here were the men from the Army Service Corp in trucks, they had been transported in trucks with their gear. But our colonel decided that we had to be strong enough to be able to carry our own packs, and we did. My companion, Sally, fell and I wasn't allowed to pick her up or anything. People just marched around her. It was terrible. We were soldiers and we were to act like soldiers.

Idyllic Yet Deadly

In July of 1943, the 1st Canadian Division invaded Sicily, attacking the German and Italian forces stationed in the town of Pachino, which marked the beginning of Operation Husky. Over the course of a year, the Canadians were able to move northward, climbing the Italian boot and entering Naples and Rome to rid the strategic airfields of German occupation.

And in turn, it was time for the CGH units to follow their countrymen into the field and move along the battle northwards behind them. As such, Elizabeth Lowe was finally on her way to Sicily. The N° 5 CGH would arrive at the shores of the Italian island and take over the main hospital in the town of Catania. She struggled with the overcrowded wards and the constant air raids as the Germans desperately tried to regain the ground they had just lost. A bombing of one of the wards that year would injure 12 RCANC nurses. The nurses had tended to men outside the hospital and lined stretchers down the alleys and under tarps (*Nursing Sisters in Sicily*, n.d.):

> During her time working at the hospital, Lowe found herself amazed at the sheer determination exhibited by the wounded soldiers, and the resilience of her colleagues, who continuously fought with being under-supplied in poor working conditions while receiving an unending supply of casualties. For the young men, returning to their units was of utmost importance. Lowe recalled a 19-year-old, with both legs shattered, expressing this sentiment. This was common among wounded Canadian men; many voiced their desire to immediately return to battle. (para. 3)

The nurses knew that these men would not be able to stand, much less be able to hold a gun and fight, but they were so proud, so delirious with blood loss and shell shock that they needed to keep on fighting and be with their men.

Over the course of that year, the N°5 CGH moved slowly behind the Canadian Divisions as they slowly took back the Italian countryside. Only in July of 1944 did the N°7 CGH arrive at the more central region of Italy, headed to the small town of Avellino, east of Naples, where Middleton worked around the clock to get her countrymen safely evacuated from the small but determined defensive hold that the Axis forces had managed over that year of the invasion.

Figure 9: A Typical Field Hospital Camp Reenactment

Middleton, who was closer to the action deep in bombing territory in central Italy, would begin to see the far more critical patients of war, from burn victims to shelled soldiers. She recalls how some had terrible injuries that disfigured them and left them immensely embarrassed. The shame was so strong that when Queen Elizabeth II paid a visit to the hospital later that year, one burn victim chose to hide in humiliation rather than let the Queen see his face.

Middleton explains how shell shock was not uncommon in the wards. Allied aircraft would set off early in the evening and fly over the hospital, causing the patients to become very anxious. Heading for Germany to bomb selected troops, they would return the next morning, once again upsetting all the patients. "Once they'd hear a plane overhead, they'd go berserk" (Florence, 2015).

Middleton and her unit would set up field hospitals close enough to the front line to receive wounded soldiers and far enough for it to be safe. The flow of patients needed to be swift and pragmatic, with injured soldiers from the battlefields and trenches ferried off behind the front line and queued up to receive triaging at the temporary hospital. Middleton's job was to address both the major and minor wounds of these soldiers and declare them ready to move onto the ambulance towards the GH.

She was always on the move. Her unit would set up mobile hospitals along the route of the front line—sometimes in fields, sometimes in deserted buildings, such as churches, schools, or hospitals in nearby towns. The FHs would send soldiers to scout new locations to set up, the soldiers would report back, and they would pack everything up and move. Efficiency was everything.

Both Middleton and Lowe made the most of their chances to visit many of Italy's small and beautiful towns during the little free time they had. Middleton recalls traveling to Rome and Florence, and even having a picnic on the top of the leaning tower of Pisa. But she also recalls how horrible it was passing so many towns which were a shell of what they once were. The bombings had devastated the towns, leaving rubble everywhere you looked. Locals walked around dazed and confused as they navigated their way through so much loss.

Moving Up and Out

Towards the end of 1944, the Italian campaign was fizzling out and the nurses and doctors were needed further up in the European theater.

Lowe's N°5 CGH had stationed itself firmly in Rome when D-Day had happened, whereas Middleton's N°7 had moved up into Holland, in a small town of Nijmegen. The fighting there was horrific, with Canadian troops arriving at the wards faster than medical staff could manage them—an endless parade of wounded soldiers, and not just Allies.

The Canadian nurses treated German soldiers too, with the understanding that these men were not enemies right then, but simply patients in need of life-saving care.

The boys who were drafted into the Nazi army were often very young and would arrive in the hospital terribly wounded, the innocence of youth still flowing in their veins. Middleton recalls (Florence, 2015):

> I remember one young German boy. I swear he must have been 15. He had an abdominal wound... he was to have nothing by mouth. And you'd turn your back, and he'd somehow gotten a little something from someone else's table. But he was a lovely little fellow, blonde, blue-eyed. He was mischievous. It was just a lark for him. (para. 50)

It was the little things, like a piece of swiped cracker, that sometimes lifted the nurses' spirits as their patients' personalities emerged during recovery. "Sometimes I inspire my patients: most often they inspire me." While this quote can't be properly attributed because its author is unknown, it's something every seasoned nurse has experienced at least once during their career. Perhaps this was Middleton's sentiment while treating this German boy—one whose future was so uncertain, but who was so obviously filled with life.

The German Nationalist Party always had one primary interest in their youth, their malleability. Per Blakemore (2017):

> It became clear that the Hitler Youth's real goal was to create more soldiers for the Reich. Children who had been saturated in Nazi ideology for years and made into obedient, fanatical soldiers. Eventually, those soldiers became younger and younger. Starting in 1943, all boys 17 and older were forced to serve in the military. (para. 13)

And from the nurses' accounts, recruitment started even younger. Hearing stories about children dying in the war due to civilian casualties is horrendous, but hearing them die in the name of a country that treated them as expendable is criminal.

Middleton remembers the emotionally draining experience of having to watch young German boys die in her ward, unaware of the true meaning of their sacrifice and the pain they were leaving their families back home.

"Some of them were so seriously wounded that they couldn't even move, and we became quite fond of them. They were only kids. The thing to me that hurt so much was that they were so young" says Middleton tearing up (Florence, 2015).

The war was coming to an end in 1945 and V-E Day was proclaimed in May of that year. This might have been the end of the war in Europe, but it was not the end of Middleton or Lowe's work. The nurses of WWII were always the final unit to leave.

It was not uncommon to find nurses from one unit transferring to another; for instance, nurses from the N°5 were transferred to the N°7 so that they could assist in the final European defense of the Battle of the Bulge. The last of the Allied and Axis soldiers needed to be stabilized, treated, and sent to a GH. The Germans were either released or kept as POWs, and the Allies were finally heading back home. Bodies needed to be collected and identified, which fell to a specialized unit established by each Allied government.

Sadly, thousands were left unidentified. Some were injured beyond recognition, others never found. There were rows and rows of bodies under white sheets, just waiting to be identified, both from FH grounds and where they died in the battle. The grave registration units within the main Allied branches followed the battle as well to monitor who and how many had died.

Middleton and her unit moved from Holland down into Germany after the victory and were now working in the Oldenburg Hospital. They stayed there for two months or so before eventually jumping on a ship called the *Rotterdam* and heading home to sweet, sweet Canada.

Lowe had already sailed back to England a few months earlier from her post in Rome. She was married to a certain Major James Bruce Lawson and returned to England to be with him before they would sail back to Canada together. Sadly, he was killed that same year in Italy defending the Gothic line, leaving her to return to Canada widowed.

… And Back Again

By 1945, both women were back home safe and sound.

The next year and a bit would be one of great demobilization, reducing the RCMAC to a core number of permanent staff and clearing up the last of the units within Europe and Asia

"Nursing sisters, like servicemen, were set adrift to find their way in a peacetime Canada" as many were not too sure where they would head out to from here (Abra, 2012). Some remained in the forces, while others drifted away to begin the lives they were supposed to have led before the war broke out.

Jessie Lee, now 31 years old, married her longtime boyfriend, Frederick Turner Middleton, whom she had met years earlier in service, and hosted the ceremony in her hometown of Murrayville. As many did before her, once she got engaged, she retired from her nursing career to focus on being a mother of two, Bob and Kathy, as well as a loving and dutiful wife.

Because of her husband's work as a high school superintendent, the family would travel around Canada for some time before finally settling down in 1974 in the town of Abbotsford, British Columbia. There she would live for the next 40 years while volunteering extensively at the Abbotsford Hospice Society.

Frederick passed away in 1982 after 35 years of marriage, which did not stop this widow from traveling as much as possible (Jessie Annie Middleton, 2019):

> Whether it was through BC to visit family, across Canada to reunite with her fellow RCAMC nursing sisters, or around the world on a church-organized tour, Jessie always came home from her journeys with the addresses of new friends she had made, many of whose names could be found in the guest books she kept on the side table in her home. (para. 1)

In July of 2012, Middleton was honored by the British when she was presented with the Queen Elizabeth II Diamond Jubilee Medal. In the same year, she was interviewed extensively by Warren Sommer, who donated 10 cassettes of this aural record of her life to the Langley Centennial Museum, Canada. Her interview concludes with a message to young people, to focus on what is important in life, to remember that our actions affect everyone, and that war is never a solution. Surely most of our front line nurses, who patched up and healed the casualties of war, must have drawn a similar conclusion. Such simple yet profound advice, gained from her experience of the war years and leading such a long post-war life. (Sommer, 2012).

*Figure 10: Jessie Middleton
Holding a Picture of Her Younger Self*

In 2019, Jessie Annie Lee Middleton passed away at the outstanding age of 102. She outlived 11 siblings and is survived by her children, grandchildren, and great-grandchildren.

With regards to our hero Elizabeth Lowe, she stayed very quiet after the war. What we do know is that in 1983 she was awarded the Florence Nightingale medal by the International Committee of the Red Cross, which is one of the highest distinctions a nurse can be awarded.

What we initially notice about these two women is surely their brilliant performance through the efforts in the British, Mediterranean, and Northern European theaters of war. But perhaps more noteworthy is in the relationships they built with their sisters, doctors, and medics over those five years together.

Middleton would go on to proclaim that "serving in the Canadian Army was the greatest privilege for me. The friendships formed a camaraderie over the years that have enriched my life greatly" (Sommer, 2013).

Lowe and Middleton were brave yet demure. They resolutely showed their strength in times of crisis. We might never know if our two heroines ever crossed paths in their wartime careers, but if they did, we know that there would have been a deep-seated understanding between them, something that those who have never experienced the horrors of war cannot truly relate to. Yet we try, by researching, listening, reading, and watching as many stories as we can, so that their accounts of life, death, and everything in between can be acknowledged and brought forward truthfully into contemporary life.

Conclusion

To do what nobody else will do, in a way that nobody else can, in spite of all we go through; is to be a nurse. —Rawsi Williams

Rawsi Williams is a present-day army nurse veteran and attorney. She is an African American woman of many talents and achievements who attributes the strength she built later in life to her early nurse training.

Williams's account of the impact nursing had on her life resonates strongly with what her predecessors in WWII shared. Nursing shaped their characters and changed the course of their lives. Whether a nurse served on the front lines of WWII in the 1940s, in Afghanistan in the 2000s, or today in any number of crises, the goal is still the same: Healing rather than killing, reviving those whose lives were nearly extinguished in the name of war.

This was their magic in WWII—they healed and restored dignity irrespective of sex, race, culture, enemy status, or political differences—and their legacy lives on. One major difference today is that we are more socially aware and better able to address the complex psychological problems caused by warfare, such as PTSD and depression. Today, women and men have regular access to mental health care after the atrocities they witnessed in their active service postings. Stigma around receiving mental health care and medication to help with symptoms is still an issue, but it is nowhere near as taboo as it was after WWI and WWII.

In WWII, the studies of such conditions were limited and superficial; the specialists were just beginning to scratch the surface through group therapy. Shell shock, neurosis, or battle fatigue were usually scribbled down on their medical records as a standard diagnosis of war, with many women and men not acknowledging their fundamental trauma and its impacts. They carried on with their lives, living with nightmares, anxiety, and overall avoidance behavior as baggage that they *thought* they had to endure.

Allied troops and medics left Europe and the Pacific en masse between 1945 and 1946, also known as Homecoming or the Great Demobilization. As you can imagine, thousands of men and women returning from overseas, all with varying degrees of unavoidable mental health struggles, caused great stress on marital relationships, families, and post-war careers.

Imagine the joy and excitement of seeing a war end, returning home to your loved ones, to a soft bed and warm house. It may have seemed like more than enough to make those nurses smile and be grateful. Now contrast that with this immense backlog of gruesome and heartbreaking images and intense emotions that veterans' minds and bodies were unable to process due to their surroundings. The repercussions in later years were immense. Countless stories of WWII nurses today depict a frail woman who will not or cannot detail or always explain how the war affected her psyche. She avoids thoughts of death and sometimes brushes it off as a symptom of the times.

The men who fought these battles with their own two hands and saw their friends die were obviously affected too. And being men and soldiers, they were expected to repress strong emotions—especially fear and sadness. Talking about feelings was just something a grown man in the 1940s didn't do, whereas the women could speak up a bit more freely and delve into pieces of their lived truth.

Perhaps the most difficult aspect of reentry for both genders was that people who had not experienced active service could never possibly comprehend the veteran's experiences. Many returning nurses suffered from an acute sense of dislocation on coming home; nothing seemed to have changed, and local people seemed uninterested in their difficult experiences and were still caught up in their humdrum concerns.

The lack of understanding by those who stayed at home became all too clear when veteran soldiers and nurses would, for example, read out the casualty list in their newspapers in real distress, only to be superficially sympathized with and sometimes outright dismissed. We cannot blame either party; perhaps we chalk it up to another casualty of war. After all that sadness and despair, people didn't want to hear it anymore; they only wanted to live joyfully and return to a "normal" that veterans could never truly regain.

When WWII ended, unfortunately so did much of the newfound respect and recognition that women had earned over those years. Many women would return to their prescribed role of housewife and mother, while many men returned to their pre-war jobs in some form or another. But with so many men fallen, post-war jobs were kept active for some women, and financial support from the governments was often provided.

Unlike many returning veterans (officers, infantrymen, supply and logistics staff, military intelligence, etc.) nurses could continue in their profession when they returned home. Although their values and perceptions had altered considerably, women who remained active in their careers came back from the war, took a short break, and then jumped right back into their duties at hospitals and clinics. As the saying goes, once a nurse, always a nurse.

When we think about the stories of Kate, Marcella, Margot, Vivian, Elizabeth, and Jessie, we can hear the songs of sisterhood. They experienced it all together—dirt, blood, hunger, cold, shame and sorrow, hope, love, empathy, companionship, and teamwork. The song they sing today (those few who remain alive) is one of humble pride. Hear them say, "We were not heroes, we just did our job."

Those long years of service provided something else for these women that others at home may not have taken advantage of due to societal pressure. The nurses had time to grow apart from the influence of a male father or husband figure in their life. Military nurses started their marriages and families much later than the rest of their peers. During the war period, they had focused instead on a career and personal growth that would bring greater emotional maturity and self-respect at a younger age than their counterparts.

Looking through Western society's lens today, we see that women are more at ease breaking with conventional gender roles and saying "no." They can choose to veer away from the traditional family life that their mothers and grandmothers espoused before them.

Following the example of our frontline nurses, women today can be ambitious and pursue fulfilling work, a professional career, travel, adventure, and camaraderie outside the domestic sphere.

The women in this book were the standard-bearers. The double meaning of this term is why it's so fitting for our heroes. According to Merriam-Webster, the term has a military connotation— "one who bears a standard or banner"—and a meaning geared towards political reform or a specific cause — "one that leads an organization, movement, or party" (2020).

They started their journey to war with the ideals of any young woman in the 1940s, yet they left it stronger and prouder for their struggle. The women imprisoned in camps experienced ordeals that would lead them to question the levels of power wielded by the patriarchy in a male-dominated world order. Their survival against all odds gave them a right to use their voices—with messages that could not be taken away when the war was over. The horrors and human suffering that nurses were exposed to forged in them a steely disposition, perseverance, and accountability in the face of hardship.

The female role in society was truly altered as a result of these women—the lessons they taught their children and still teach us today as we read about their lives, losses, struggles, and accomplishments.

How do their stories of bravery speak to the courage that we all need today? The public perception of the nursing profession changed again, suddenly and dramatically, in 2020 with the outbreak of the Coronavirus pandemic. Suddenly, nurses worldwide were being publicly applauded for their work on the front lines and called heroes.

Anonymous British street artist Banksy donated a work of art to the Southampton General Hospital in the UK that depicts a young boy playing with a superhero doll called SuperNurse, complete with a nurse's cape, and an apron with the Red Cross emblem—the only item in color. The boy has discarded his Batman and Spiderman dolls. It remains to be seen whether this new respect for the work of nurses will lead to an upgrade in pay and status.

Our Angels of Mercy, Nightingales, and Bluebirds were tough, pragmatic women who had to be brave, patient, encouraging, and positive before injured and broken men. Hiding their own pain and suffering was required, but opening up to their fellow sisters and colleagues was also important. Sharing their fears and regrets, their hopes and dreams, was what got most of them through the war alive. It's an inspirational lesson for all the women and men who are reading these final words.

What we should notice clearly about nurses—those in WWII and those today—is not their singular courage, but rather their *shared* bravery. These women were rarely ever alone—they cried, smiled, laughed, and mourned together. This makes one thing abundantly apparent: Unity for change is far easier and healthier than change through violence.

Credit is due to you, the reader, for your interest in this less-explored area of wartime history. If you liked what you just read, please leave a review and say what you took from this book or how it made you feel.

International Nurses Day is marked on the 12th of May. Find some time to speak to other women and men who lived through and fought in a war; take a minute to listen to their stories with renewed compassion, vigor, and interest.

The events of the Second World War are slipping into the past as those who lived through it become fewer in number, but the individuals, their stories, and the lessons contained within them must never be forgotten.

Author

Elise Baker has had a lifelong interest in women's history and WWII. Her immediate family, from the borderlands of the Czech Republic, became stateless refugees and dispersed all over the world after the Second World War. Their riveting stories and Elise's mixed European heritage inspired a deep interest in this historical period. Elise is especially passionate about excavating the past to unearth the stories of women whose remarkable feats and accomplishments have been buried and forgotten because of their gender.

She holds a Bachelor of Arts degree in Humanities with a specialty in English Literature and a Postgraduate Diploma in Information Management. Her professional career has been in libraries and archives, and subsequently in television, in an editorial capacity. Elise is also a keen reader of both literary fiction and biographies, and she appreciates the variety of genres that makes history come alive to readers in exciting, accessible, and relatable ways.

If you have enjoyed reading this book, it would be greatly appreciated if you would be so kind as to take a moment to leave a review. For more books in the Brave Women Who Changed the Course of World War II Series please visit: **www.ReadEliseBaker.com**

References

Abra, G. J. (2012). *Prairie bluebirds: The no. 5 Canadian General Hospital nurses at war* [Master's thesis, The University of Manitoba]. University of Manitoba Libraries. https://mspace.lib.umanitoba.ca/bitstream/handle/1993/5271/Abra_Glennis.pdf?sequence=1&isAllowed=y

African American nurses in World War II. (2019, July 8). National Women's History Museum. https://www.womenshistory.org/articles/african-american-nurses-world-war-ii

American Legion HQ. (2014, December 19). *Battle of the Bulge remembered: Kate Nolan* [Video]. YouTube. https://www.youtube.com/watch?v=ilQ7VlNq6cA

American Veterans Center. (2020, February 20). *Marcella LeBeau, nurse at D-Day and Battle of the Bulge (Full Interview)* [Video]. YouTube. https://www.youtube.com/watch?v=th5D7_K_ZKI

The Army Nurse Corps. (2014, December 18). U.S. Army Center for Military History. https://history.army.mil/books/wwii/72-14/72-14.HTM

Australians in World War II. (n.d.). AWM London; Department of Veterans' Affairs. https://www.awmlondon.gov.au/ australians-in-wwii

Atwood, K. (2019). Women Heroes of World War II: 32 Stories of Espionage, Sabotage, Resistance, and Rescue. Chicago Review Press.

Bates, C. Dodd, D.E. & Rousseau, N. [editors] (2005). On All Frontiers: Four Centuries of Canadian Nursing. University of Ottawa Press.

Bissland, E. (2022, April 23). *WWII nurse Lieutenant Colonel Vivian Bullwinkel's incredible tale of survival.* ABC News. https://www.abc.net.au/news/ 2022-04-24/wwii-nurse-lieutenant-colonel- vivian-bullwinkel/101005050

Blakemore, E. (2017, December 11). *How the Hitler youth turned a generation of kids into Nazis.* History.com; A&E Television Networks. https://www.history.com/news/how-the- hitler-youth-turned-a-generation-of-kids-into- nazis

Bluebirds. (n.d.). Valour Canada. https://valourcanada.ca/military-history- library/bluebirds/

Bowden, J. & Barclay, T. (2015). *Nurses at war: The true story of army nursing sisters' courage in World War II.* Wyndham Books. In *Amazon.* https://www.amazon.com/Nurses-War-Nursing-Sisters-Courage-ebook/dp/B017F0JSZA

Brigadier Margot Turner DBE, RRC (1910–1993). (n.d.). Big Red Book. https://www.bigredbook.info/margot_turner.html

Britannica, T. Editors of Encyclopaedia (2021, August 1). *Prisoner of war.* Encyclopedia Britannica. https://www.britannica.com/topic/prisoner-of-war

Canadian women in the World Wars. (n.d.). Military Wiki. https://military-history.fandom.com/wiki/Canadian_women_in_the_World_Wars#Canadian_Women.27s_Army_Corps

Brooks Tomblin, B. (2003). G.I. Nightingales: The Army Nurse Corps in World War II. (University Press of Kentucky).

Canada's WW2 Nursing Sisters. (2015, November 24). All about Canadian history. https://cdnhistorybits.wordpress.com/2015/11/24/canadas-ww2-nursing-sisters/

Cizik School of Nursing, University of Texas. (2017, February 24). *Caring corrupted - The killing nurses of the Third Reich* [Video]. YouTube. https://www.youtube.com/watch?v=Rz8ge4aw8Ws

Dame Margot Turner. (n.d.). Never Such Innocence. https://www.neversuchinnocence.com/dame-margot-turner-people-profiles-military-medicine-second-world-war

Dame Margot Turner. (n.d.). QARANC. https://www.qaranc.co.uk/damemargotturner.php

Eder, M. K. (2021). *The Girls Who Stepped Out of Line: Untold Stories of the Women Who Changed the Course of World War II. In Google Books.* https://books.google.co.za/books?id=A_ceEAAAQBAJ&printsec=frontcover#v=onepage&q&f=false

Eder, M. K. (2020, May 25). Memorial Day reminder: In pandemic, as in war, nurses serve bravely at the front. *USA Today.* https://www.usatoday.com/story/opinion/2020/05/25/coronavirus-pandemic-war-nurses-serve-front-memorial-day-column/5236109002/

Engleman, M.P. (2008). Mission Accomplished: Stop the Clock. iUniverse.

Fessler, D. B. (1996). *No time for fear: Voices of American military nurses in World War II*. Michigan State University Press. In *Amazon*. https://www.amazon.com/ No-Time-Fear-American-Military- ebook/dp/B00VFU2RXC?asin= B00VFU2RXC&revisionId= 8c9fe9a6&format=1&depth=1. Excerpts in *Encyclopedia.com*. https://www.encyclopedia.com/history/ educational-magazines/world-war-ii- nurses#:~:text=Sixteen%20nurses%20 were%20killed%20during

Fifteen famous nursing quotes to start your career (n.d.) RN Programs. https://www.rnprograms.org/articles/ 15-famous-nursing-quotes-to-inspire-your- career.htm

Fifty Australians - Sister Vivian Bullwinkel. (2016). Australian War Memorial. https://www.awm.gov.au/visit/exhibitions/ fiftyaustralians/5

Florence, E. (2015, June 17). *Nursing Sister healed the wounds of war*. Elinor Florence. https://www.elinorflorence.com/blog/ canadian-nurses-wartime/

Giles, N. (2016, August 10). *Dame Margot Turner: From nurse to FEPOW*. Forces War Records. https://www.forces-war- records.co.uk/blog/2016/08/10/dame-margot- turner- from-nurse-to-fepow

Gompertz, W. (2020, May 6). *New Banksy artwork appears at Southampton hospital.* BBC News. https://www.bbc.com/news/entertainment-arts-52556544

Groves, S. (2021, November 23). *Marcella LeBeau, WWII nurse and tribal leader, dies at 102.* Military Times. https://www.militarytimes.com/military-honor/salute-veterans/2021/11/23/marcella-lebeau-wwii-nurse-and-tribal-leader-dies-at-102/

Heywood, A. (2002, December 9). *Australian Army Nursing Service (AANS) (1902–1948).* The Australian Women's Register. https://www.womenaustralia.info/biogs/AWE0408b.htm

Haskell, R.G. (2017). Helmets and Lipstick: An Army Nurse in World War II. Enhanced Media Publishing.

Hitchcock, M. (2018, August 13). *Short history of military nursing: U.S. Cadet Nurse Corps.* Ebling Library of University of Wisconsin - Madison. https://researchguides.library.wisc.edu/c.php?g=860714&p=6167910

Howard, H. (2020, May 21). *Our WWII story: Nurse shares cold memories of treating the wounded in tents.* The American Legion. https://www.legion.org/honor/249079/our-wwii-story-nurse-shares-cold-memories-treating-wounded-tents

Hudson, M. (2019, September 16). Wounded Knee
      Massacre: United States History [1890].
      In *Encyclopædia Britannica.*
      https://www.britannica.com/event/
      Wounded-Knee-Massacre

*Information about the Prisoners of War of the Japanese
      1939-1945.* (n.d.). Forces War Records.
      https://www.forces-war-
      records.co.uk/prisoners-of-war-of-the-
      japanese-1939- 1945#Sumatra

Iowa PBS. (2015, September 14). *Experiences of a female
      nurse during World War II* [Video]. YouTube.
      https://www.youtube.com/watch?v=
      CyJmek20QSA

Jacoby, A. (2022, March 21). *25 Inspirational Quotes
      About Being A Nurse.* Medelita.
      https://www.medelita.com/blog/
      best-inspirational-nurse-quotes

Jakubenko, K. (2021, May 12). *Vivian Bullwinkel:
      Australian nurse, war hero, legend.* My Tributes.
      https://www.mytributes.com.au/article/
      vivian-bullwinkel/4256659/

Jensen, A. (2016, January 25). *Sexual healing: nurses,
      gender, and Victorian era intimacy.* The Gettysburg
      Compiler.
      https://gettysburgcompiler.org/2016/01/25/
      sexual-healing-nurses-gender-and-victorian-era-
      intimacy/

Jessie Annie Middleton (nee Lee). (2019, May 22).
   The Abbotsford News.
   https://www.abbynews.com/obituaries/
   jessie-annie-middleton-nee-lee/

Kuhn, B. (1999). *Angels of Mercy: The Army Nurses
   of World War II.* Aladdin.

Lawrence, S. (2021, May 12). *The legacy of the world's most
   famous nurse, Florence Nightingale.* British Heritage.
   https://britishheritage.com/history/legacy-
   worlds-famous-nurse-florence-nightingale

Legacy Marcella LeBeau. (2006). South Dakota
   Hall of Fame.
   https://sdexcellence.org/Marcella_LeBeau_
   2006

Marcella LeBeau. (2021, December 1).
   Timber Lake Topic.
   https://www.timberlakesouthdakota.com/
   obituaries/marcella-lebeau-0

Marcella LeBeau. (2022, January 2). In *Wikipedia.*
   https://en.wikipedia.org/wiki/
   Marcella_LeBeau

Margot Turner. (2022, April 26). In *Wikipedia.*
   https://en.wikipedia.org/wiki/Margot_Turner

Marsh, J. H. (2012, February 23). *Japanese Canadian internment: Prisoners in their own country.* The Canadian Encyclopedia. https://www.thecanadianencyclopedia.ca/en/article/japanese-internment-banished-and-beyond-tears-feature

McAllister, M. (2014). Vivian Bullwinkel: A model of resilience and a symbol of strength. *Collegian*, 22(1), 135–141. https://www.academia.edu/11982190/Vivian_Bullwinkel_A_model_of_resilience_and_a_symbol_of_strength

McBryde, B. (1985). Quiet Heroines: Nurses of the Second World War. Cakebreads Publications.

McKie, L. (2020, November 20). *Marcella LeBeau neé Ryan.* The Log Book Project. https://thelogbookproject.com/marcella-lebeau-nee-ryan/

Merriam-Webster. (2020). Merriam-Webster's collegiate dictionary (11th ed.).

The New Brunswick Museum celebrates National Nursing Week with this blog dedicated to 100+ years of the Nursing Association of New Brunswick. (2019, May 10). The New Brunswick Museum. https://www.nbm-mnb.ca/the-new-brunswick-museum-celebrates-national-nursing-week-with-this-blog-dedicated-to-100-years-of-the-nursing-association-of-new-brunswick/

Monahan, E & Neidel-Greenlee, R. (2004). And If I
　　　　Perish: Frontline U.S. Army Nurses in World
　　　　War II. Anchor Books.

Mortimer, B. (2013). Sisters: Extraordinary True-Life
　　　　Stories from Nurses in World War Two. Arrow.

Nuclear Vault. (2009, August 16). *The army nurse (1945)*
　　　　[Video]. YouTube.
　　　　https://www.youtube.com/watch?v=
　　　　0kWcbzOxXxQ

Nunn, G. (2019, April 18). *Bangka Island: The WW2
　　　　massacre and a "truth too awful to speak."* BBC
　　　　News. https://www.bbc.com/news/
　　　　world-australia-47796046

Nursing and medicine during World War II. (2014,
　　　　December 14). CEUfast Nursing CE.
　　　　https://ceufast.com/blog/nursing-and-
　　　　medicine-during-world-war-ii#:~:text=
　　　　World%20War%20II%20brought%20nurses

Nursing Sisters in Sicily (1943). (n.d.). Valour Canada.
　　　　https://valourcanada.ca/military-history-
　　　　library/nursing-sisters-in-sicily-1943/

The Nursing Sisters of Canada (2017).
　　　　Veterans Affairs Canada.
　　　　https://www.veterans.gc.ca/eng/remembrance
　　　　/those-who-served/women-veterans/nursing-
　　　　sisters

Parry, J. F. (2015). *Joyce's war: The Second World War journal of a Queen Alexandra nurse* (R. Evans, Ed.). The History Press.

Pledge of the U.S. Army Nurse, World War II. (2007, December 8). Sedulia's Quotations. https://sedulia.blogs.com/sedulias_quotations/2007/12/pledge-of-the-u.html

QA World War Two Nursing. (n.d.). QARANC. https://www.qaranc.co.uk/qa_world_war_two_nursing.php

Queen Alexandra's Royal Army Nursing Corps. (2021, May 10). *Brigadier Dame Evelyn Marguerite Turner, DBE, RRC* [Video]. YouTube. https://www.youtube.com/watch?v=a7veisfiHtg

Review by Mark Bathhurst of Anna Rogers' While You're Away: New Zealand Nurses at War 1899-1948 (Auckland University Press, 2003) https://www.nzgeo.com/stories/new-zealands-nightingales/

Rust, J. (2019, October 16). 100 years young: Marcella LeBeau joined by family and friends near and far for celebration. *West River Eagle.* https://www.westrivereagle.com/articles/100-years-young-marcella-lebeau-joined-by-family-and-friends-near-and-far-for-celebration/

The Second World War. (2015, December 1). *Black women serve as nurses in World War II* [Video]. YouTube. https://www.youtube.com/watch?v=-dq1uRyya4U

Sandilands, J. (1993, October 11). Obituary: Dame Margot Turner. *The Independent.* https://www.independent.co.uk/news/people/obituary-dame-margot-turner-1510255.html

Sex overseas: "What Soldiers Do" complicates WWII history. (2013, May 31). NPR. https://www.wnyc.org/story/296418-sex-overseas-what-soldiers-do-complicates-wwii-history/

Smith, G. (2007, September 30). A sister in WW II's band of brothers. *Chicago Tribune.* https://www.chicagotribune.com/news/ct-xpm-2007-10-01-0709300640-story.html

Smyth, S. J. (1986). *The will to live: The story of Dame Margot Turner, D.B.E., R.R.C.* In *Internet Archive.* https://archive.org/details/willtolivestoryo00smyt/page/n7/mode/2up

Sommer, W. (2012, Interview of Jessie Lee Middleton. Interviews took place March 26 to August 21, 2012.) 10 cassettes donated to Langley Centennial Museum. https://museum.tol.ca/museum/Portal/explore.aspx?lang=en-US

Sommer, W. (2013, November 6). Healing hands
and a heavy heart. *The Langley Times*. In Issuu.
https://issuu.com/blackpress/docs/
i20131107070550186

Stamberg, S. (2004, May 28). *Kate Nolan, WWII
combat nurse.* NPR.
https://www.npr.org/2004/05/28/1913743/
kate-nolan-wwii-combat-nurse

Stamberg, S. (2007, September 24). *Mother, son
share experiences of war.* NPR.
https://www.npr.org/2007/09/24/14627960/
mother-son-share-experiences-of-war

Starns, P. (2010). *Surviving Tenko: The story of Margot
Turner.* History Press.

Sundin, S. (2018a, October 8). *Army nursing in World
War II - Training and rank.* Sarah Sundin.
https://www.sarahsundin.com/army-nursing-
in-world-war-ii-training-and-rank/

Sundin, S. (2018b, October 15). *Army nursing
in World War II - Uniforms.* Sarah Sundin.
https://www.sarahsundin.com/army-nursing-
in-world-war-ii-uniforms/

Sundin, S. (2018c, October 1). *Army nursing in
World War II - Who could serve.* Sarah Sundin.
https://www.sarahsundin.com/army-nursing-
in-world-war-ii-requirements/

Taylor, E. (1999). *Combat Nurse* Robert Hale Ltd.

Timeline - World History Documentaries. (2018, August 30). *Angels of Mercy* [Video]. YouTube. https://www.youtube.com/watch?v= zGS0xWaVDEM

Tribute for Katherine M. Nolan. (2019). Fuller Funeral Home-Cremation Service. https://www.fullernaples.com/tributes/ Katherine-Nolan

The Untold Past. (2022, March 18). *The brutal executions of the nurses of Bangka Island* [Video]. YouTube. https://www.youtube.com/watch?v= sIbZD7XDCvM

Toman, C. (2008) An Officer and a Lady: Canadian Military Nursing and the Second World War. UBC Press.

Tyrer, N. (2008) Sisters in Arms: British Army Nurses Tell Their Story. Weidenfeld & Nicolson.

Vivian Bullwinkel. (2019, December 26). In *Wikipedia*. https://en.wikipedia.org/wiki/Vivian_ Bullwinkel

Waln, V. (2021, November 26). *Marcella LeBeau filled lives with "love and significant meaning."* Indian Country Today. https://indiancountrytoday.com/news/ marcella-lebeau-filled-lives-with-love-and- significant-meaning

Women in the military. (2021, July 14).
Lambton County Museums.
https://www.lambtonmuseums.ca/en/
lambton-heritage-museum/women-in-the-
military.aspx#World-War-II

WW2 military hospitals. (n.d.). WW2 US Medical
Research Centre.
https://www.med-dept.com/articles/ww2-
military-hospitals-general- introduction/

Wandrey, J. (2015) Bedpan Commando: The Story
of a Combat Nurse During World War II.
Amazon Kindle Edition.

Zinn, C. (2000, July 17). Vivian Bullwinkel: Australian
nursing sister who was sole survivor of wartime
massacre. *The Guardian.*
https://www.theguardian.com/news/2000/
jul/17/guardianobituaries

Image References

Figure 1. *First Lieutenant Kathryn (Flynn) Nolan, US Army Nurse Corps, World War II* [Image]. (n.d.). Women in Military Service for America Memorial Foundation, Inc. See Acknowledgments section for permission.

Figure 2. *Marcella Rose Ryan in 1944* [Image]. (1944). See Acknowledgments section for permission. https://thelogbookproject.com/marcella-lebeau-nee-ryan/

Figure 3. Scofield, W. (2018, February 7). *Surgical tools in Field Hospital* [Image]. https://unsplash.com/photos/TjfQR3JgGG8

Figure 4. Australian War Memorial. (1914–1918). *Nursing Sister in typical QAIMNS uniform with badges, 1914-1918* [Image]. https://www.awm.gov.au/collection/C1120870

Figure 5. *Dame Margot Turner wearing tropical kit alongside an Indian elephant* [Image]. (n.d.). Trustees of the Army Medical Services Museum. See Acknowledgments section for permission.

Figure 6. Australian War Memorial. (1941, May). *Studio portrait of Staff Nurse Vivian Bullwinkel, Australian Army Nursing Service (AANS)* [Image]. https://www.awm.gov.au/collection/C1002881

Figure 7. Australian War Memorial. (n.d.).
　　　Rescued POWs from the 2/10th and 2/13th
　　　ANS units, 1945 [Image].
　　　https://www.awm.gov.au/collection/C14450

Figure 8. Australian War Memorial. (1945, September).
　　　Informal group portrait of AANS homecoming,
　　　Sister Bullwinkel second from the left [Image].
　　　https://www.awm.gov.au/collection/C50962

Figure 9. Australian War Memorial. (1946). *Captain*
　　　Vivian Bullwinkel sitting witness at the War Crimes
　　　Tribunal, 1946 [Image].
　　　https://www.awm.gov.au/collection/C1085804

Figure 10. *Young Jessie Middleton in her Bluebird uniform*
　　　image. (n.d.). Middleton Family. See
　　　Acknowledgments section for permission.

Figure 11. Brooks, S. (2018, November 24).
　　　A typical Field Hospital camp reenactment [Image].
　　　https://unsplash.com/photos/
　　　KYqVQv0V4uw

Figure 12. *Jessie Middleton holding a picture of her younger self*
　　　image [Image]. (n.d.). Elinor Florence.
　　　See Acknowledgments section for permission.
　　　https://www.elinorflorence.com/blog/
　　　canadian-nurses-wartime/

Acknowledgments

Thank you to the **Women in Military Service for America Memorial Foundation Inc.** for permission to use the image of Katherine Flynn Nolan. Permission granted in writing on 10 May 2022.

Thank you to the **Middleton family**, especially granddaughter Amanda Morganton, for permission to use the image of younger Jessie Middleton in uniform.

And thank you to **Elinor Florence** (https://www.elinorflorence.com/blog/wartime-women/) for her kind permission to use the image of senior Jessie Middleton holding a picture of her younger self, as well as for her inspirational **Wartime Wednesdays blog**: https://www.elinorflorence.com/blog/category/wartime-wednesdays/

Thank you to the **BC History of Nursing Society** for the oral history resources on their website: https://www.bcnursinghistory.ca/

Thank you to the **Australian War Memorial** for their permission to those images from their website in the public domain—in this case, those of the Australian Army Nurses Corps (AANS).

Thank you to the **Museum of Military Medicine** for their Archive Service's permission to use the image of Dame Margot Turner with elephant in Malaya. Permission granted on 23 May 2022.

Thank you to the **LeBeau family**, especially Marcella's daughter Gerri, for permission to use the image of younger Marcella in uniform. Special thanks to **Nicholas Devaux** of **The Log Book Project** for all his help and support in procuring permission, as well as for the marvelous resources within his project, particularly the signee page on Marcella LeBeau by Lars McKie. **https://thelogbookproject.com/**

Other Books by Elise Baker

**Women Code Breakers: The Best Kept Secret
of WWII**
*True Stories of Female Code Breakers Whose Top-Secret Work
Helped Win WWII*

Princess, Countess, Socialite, Spy
True Stories of High-Society Ladies Turned WWII Spies

Women Rescuers of WWII
*True stories of the unsung women heroes who rescued refugees
and Allied servicemen in WWII*

Printed in Great Britain
by Amazon